A CODE-BREAKER'S TALE

A CODE-BREAKERS TALE

Hugh Melinsky

With illustrations by
Renate Melinsky

Larks Press

Published by the Larks Press
Ordnance Farm House, Guist Bottom,
Dereham, Norfolk NR20 5PF

Tel./Fax 01328 829207

Printed at the Lanceni Press, Fakenham, Norfolk

British Library Cataloguing-in-Publication Data.
A catalogue record for this book is available from the
British Library.

ISBN 0 948400 70 6

For
our grandchildren

Imogen and Robin

Thomas and Jessie

Elizabeth and Thomas

CAMP-SITE ON MOROTAI
Sketched by the author

Introduction

This little book started life as an account for my grandchildren of my wartime experiences in the Far East, especially because that part of the war is little known in England. For wider publication, however, some of the background has been filled in so that the work of the Australian Wireless Units can be better appreciated in the context of the war in the South West Pacific Area.

Some of this information I did not know at the time because a basic principle of wartime intelligence was that only the most senior officers knew the whole picture; other workers had to keep to their own little pitch and were not allowed to discuss it with anyone outside their own unit. When that unit was in the 'bush' in the Northern Territory of Australia or on a remote Pacific island it was difficult to find out what was going on in the world outside. We relied largely on the B.B.C. News.

For this further detail I am particularly indebted to Jack Bleakley's *The Eavesdroppers* and Alan Stripp's *Codebreaker in the Far East*, though the latter deals more with South East Asia Command than with the South West Pacific Area. For obvious reasons all those working in military intelligence were sworn to lifelong secrecy, and so very few personal records survive. In recent years, however, the official restrictions for that period have been largely though not completely lifted, and so this tale may now be told.

Throughout my time overseas I wrote home to my family about once a week, and my parents kept all my letters and I still have them. In Australia for the first few months we were limited to one 'airgraph' a week: this was a single sheet which was photographed and the negatives flown home, thus saving a lot of weight. A small positive of each was developed in England and delivered. A specimen is reproduced below. All letters were censored and we could give no hint of what we were doing or even where we were.

After September 1944 we were allowed one air-letter form

a week which gave rather more space. A year later, when the war was finished, restrictions were lifted and we could write ordinary letters fairly freely. So the framework of my story is reliable, though I cannot vouch for the accuracy of every detail. Fifty years ago is a long time to remember.

Norwich, 1998   Hugh Melinsky

CONTENTS

WHITGIFT SCHOOL, CROYDON

CHAPTER 1

Learning Japanese

I never intended to learn Japanese, or go out to the Far East. Come to that, I never intended to join the army. My main interest was in aeroplanes and flying, and that indicated the Air Force. In 1942 I was eighteen and in the sixth form at Whitgift School, Croydon. The war had been going on for two and a half years and the Royal Air Force had lost a lot of pilots and aircrew. A senior officer came round to the school to recruit some new ones, and I, with half a dozen others, asked for an interview. I remember his asking me some mathematical questions, most of which I got wrong, but that did not seem to matter too much because at the end he handed me a piece of paper stating that I was an accepted volunteer for aircrew duties (pilot), subject to a medical examination. I had to produce this form when I was called up at nineteen.

I won an Exhibition to Cambridge in classics and I was allowed to go up for a year because the university was nearly empty. Most of the friends I made there were either conscientious objectors or medically unfit - one of the latter died in 1996 at the age of seventy-five!

I went up in October 1942 at a time when the war in and around Europe was beginning to turn in our favour: before then we had won no victories; after then we suffered no defeats. In that month the German and Italian forces in north Africa were beaten at Alamein, in Egypt, and in Russia the vast German armies were held at Stalingrad, so Hitler's plan to surround the Mediterranean, in the north through Russia and in the south through Palestine, came to nothing. The Japanese planned to break through Burma into India and meet up with Hitler in the Middle East, but they suffered their first major defeat on June 4th, 1942, in the great naval battle of Midway when they lost four of their best aircraft-carriers along with their planes and aircrews. It was the first sea battle to have been fought and won entirely by ship-borne aircraft, and it showed the shape of things to come in the Pacific.

1

The air-raids on England slackened, although Norwich suffered heavy ones in April 1942, and as a prefect at school I no longer had to troop down with my thirty third-form boys to the underground shelter in the grounds when the siren sounded. Instead of heavy bombers the Germans switched to tip-and-run raids by fighters, and my closest encounter with the Luftwaffe (the German Air Force) occurred on August 13th, 1942 when the family was managing to have a holiday at Teignmouth in south Devon. We were coming back one afternoon to our guest-house from the cinema when (to quote from my diary):

'I heard a frightful racket coming from the sea. My surprise was complete when I saw the sky full of FW 190s! I yelled "Focke Wulfs: get down!" to the assembled company, and fell flat on the grass - waiting for a bullet in the back to end my days. My attention had been riveted to what looked at first like long-range tanks underneath - but we soon found out that they were nice big bombs. I saw two columns go up, but also heard things zipping into the ground all about us. In a minute or two I got up and made for a pill-box which was locked. I comforted some scared-looking females - and it was all over... Eight planes, it seems, had taken part, and presumably eight bombs.'

Of more concern to most people was the rationing of food, clothing, and petrol. Much of this had to be brought across the Atlantic from America, and in the first six months of 1942 German U-boats (submarines) sank 568 ships, more than three million tons of shipping. You can see what each person's weekly ration of food was from the table. (The points were for tinned food and also chocolate; you could not have both.) There was no bread but only a light brown 'national' loaf. Housekeeping was difficult, but nobody went hungry, and in fact the health of the nation has never been better.

The other main nuisance was the black-out, designed to mislead enemy aircraft at night. There were no street lights, and car headlamps had only a narrow slit. No light was allowed to be seen coming out of a house, and buses and trains were lit by dim blue bulbs. To make travel more confusing, all signposts were removed, in case of invasion by airborne troops. But life continued for us

2

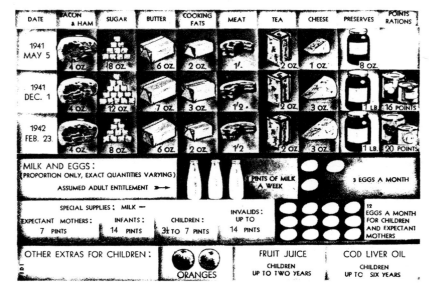

DATE	BACON & HAM	SUGAR	BUTTER	COOKING FATS	MEAT	TEA	CHEESE	PRESERVES	POINTS RATIONS
1941 MAY 5	4 OZ	8 OZ	6 OZ	2 OZ	1/-	2 OZ	1 OZ	8 OZ	
1941 DEC. 1	4 OZ	12 OZ	7 OZ	3 OZ	1/2	2 OZ	3 OZ	1 LB	16 POINTS
1942 FEB. 23	4 OZ	8 OZ	6 OZ	2 OZ	1/2	2 OZ	3 OZ	1 LB	20 POINTS

MILK AND EGGS:
(PROPORTION ONLY, EXACT QUANTITIES VARYING)

ASSUMED ADULT ENTITLEMENT ➤— 3 PINTS OF MILK A WEEK — 3 EGGS A MONTH

SPECIAL SUPPLIES : MILK —				
EXPECTANT MOTHERS: 7 PINTS	INFANTS : 14 PINTS	CHILDREN : 3½ TO 7 PINTS	INVALIDS : UP TO 14 PINTS	12 EGGS A MONTH FOR CHILDREN AND EXPECTANT MOTHERS

OTHER EXTRAS FOR CHILDREN : — ORANGES — FRUIT JUICE CHILDREN UP TO TWO YEARS — COD LIVER OIL CHILDREN UP TO SIX YEARS

remarkably normally. The family had been evacuated at the beginning of the war to the south coast, to Ferring, and later Goring, and after the invasion of France, to Wales, to Meifod, Montgomeryshire, but I stayed near Croydon with friends so that I could continue with school. My father had bought me a small motor-bike because of transport difficulties, and I was rather proud of the fact that at the end of the summer term I drove to Wales without any signposts and took only one wrong turning.

As nothing much seemed to be happening war-wise, my mother came back to Croydon in July 1940 to open up the house again, just in time for the start of the Blitz, and I followed in August. I remember standing on the railway bridge at East Croydon station watching a succession of Junkers Ju 87s dive-bombing the aerodrome about two miles away. I could distinctly see the bomb falling from each plane and then a cloud of dust from the explosion. My parents stayed there for the rest of the war.

In October 1942 I went up to Christ's College, Cambridge, for a year because I was too young to be called up for the R.A.F., and continued my study of Greek and Latin. One day in the spring of 1943, I went to my tutor to have my Greek composition marked. He sat in his comfortable chair, looking like a well-fed pussy-cat, and said, 'Oh, by the way, before we begin, would you like to learn Japanese? They are very short of people who can translate it.' I

3

nearly fell through the chair, but managed to say, 'What would I have to do?' He replied, 'You'll have to have an interview. If you're accepted you'll train for six months in this country and then probably go out to the Far East in the army.' I thought this sounded interesting and replied, 'I'm prepared to try anything once.' So I had an interview with Colonel Tiltman from the War Office department M.I.8. He asked me if I played chess, and I said I didn't; or did crossword puzzles, and I said I did; or could read music, and I said 'Reasonably'; and other questions which at the time seemed odd, but which later I understood. He said that I would hear from him, and I told him about the Air Force offer, but he said 'Don't bother about that.' So I started my summer holiday.

Half way through, on a day when I was sunbathing in the garden, a telegram arrived telling me to report to the Inter-Services Special Intelligence School at Bedford on the last day of August. So began the six months' hardest work of my life. There were thirty of us in the class (twenty-nine men and one woman) who had all done Greek and Latin at Oxford or Cambridge and so they thought we could tackle Japanese. We had two teachers. One was Captain Oswald Tuck, a retired naval officer, rather stout, with a pointed white beard. He stumped up and down the classroom as if he were on the deck of a battleship. He had served on the China station for many years before the war and could speak and write Japanese

4

東京　讀賣新聞

米國の對露援助品は今後 Archangel の航路によって送られることになる との報道は當地でも少からぬ注意を喚起して居り冬期に近づき Boston Archangel の利用價値が減少する今日何故から決定をなしたかに就て多大の疑問起し各種の臆測が行はれて居る

一部では米國の對日友好的 gesture だとなして居るも英官邊筋では露西亞が最大の援助を必要とする地點えの最短路であるために極東情勢とは何等關係ないものとなして居り更に第三說として太平洋情勢逼迫の結果米國は極東方面の米國船引揚を命じ、なるたけ危險地域に自國船を送らぬやう取計つて居るが Vladivostok 航路を避ける事も同樣の理由に基くものであらうとの解釋もある

外交消息通は恐以上の三つてき考慮に入れられて居ると見何等

(YOMIURI SHIMBUN article dated 23rd October 1941)
(から　とうせん)

. beikokuno tairoenjohinwa kongo boston archangel

nokooroni yotteokurareru kotoninaru tonohoodoo

watootidemo sukunakaranu chuuyiwo kankisiteori tookini

tikazuki archangel noriyookatiga genshoosuru konnitinaze

5 kakarukettei wonasitaka nituite tadainogimon okosi

kakushuno okusokuga okonawareteru

itibudewa beikokuno tainiti yuukooteki gesuture

datonasiterumo eikanpen sujidewa rosiⁿga saidaino

enjowohituyoo tosurutiten yenosaitan rodearu tamedekyokutoo

jooseitowa nanrakankei naimonoto nasiteori/sarani

10 daisansetu tosite taiheiyoo jooseihippaku nokekkabeikoku

wakyokutoo hoomenno beikokusen hikiagewo meijinarutake

kikentiikini jikokusenwo okuranuyoo torihakaratte yiruga

vladiostok koorowo sakerukotodmo dooyoono riyuunimoto

zukumonode arootono kaishakumoaru

gaikooshocsoku tuuwaosoraku ijoonomitu tomokooryoni

15 irerareteru tomiinanrakano katatide|tooajjooseini kankeiaru

kotowahitei dekimaitosi korenitaisuru nihonnohankyoo

wokyoomi bukakumati tutuaru

sikasitooti yuuryokusujiwa konokinioite beikokuno

daikibotainiti joohowa kangaerarezu nitibeikaidan

20 nozentowa hikantekida tokansoku kotoni eijinnimeino

taihojikenno mikaiketu nihonkookuuro timor enchootoowo

sitekinitiei kankeiwa/kiwametejuudai najootaini

narukeikoo/kosotuyokere kaizenno choowahotondo nakukakaru

nitieikankeiwa hituzen nitibeikaidan nimoeikyoo

oyobosutono ikoowo morasiteru

NOTES

1.7 yuukoo 'friendly'; YUU 24,2; KOO 38,3.
- 1.10 hippaku 'pressure', 'tenseness'.

fluently, but had little idea of how the language worked. The other was a slim young army officer who was expert at taking the language to pieces, and was also a good teacher. We called him 'Chuu-i' because that is the Japanese for 'lieutenant'. His name was Eric Ceadel.

On the first day we were issued with two Japanese-English dictionaries, one in English letters and one for characters, and given four short messages to translate. Here is one of them:

> senkyoo 00860 diahonei happyoo kuhigozen juujihan sinshoo birumahoomen teikokurikugun butaiwa pegu oyobi rangoon fukinnioite tekigunno shuryokuwo gekimetusi nanahigogo peguwo hatihi gozenjuuji rangoonwo kanzenni senryooseri.

> War situation 86. Imperial Headquarters report. 1030 on the 9th.
> In the Burma area Imperial army units have wiped out the main force of the enemy army in the region of Pegu and Rangoon, and completely occupied Pegu at 7.0 p.m. on the 7th and Rangoon at 10 a.m. on the 8th.

The Japanese do not normally write with letters as Europeans do, but with pictures called 'characters'. Every character can be pronounced in two ways, one Chinese (where the characters were invented) and one Japanese. Here is a mountain 山 with smoke coming out of the top, and it can be pronounced either 'san' or 'yama'. The famous mountain outside Tokyo is called either Fuji-san or Fuji-yama, written with three characters meaning 'not two mountains' or 'no other mountain like it'. A Japanese book starts at the back because they write from right to left and from top to bottom. The previous pages show some writing I did with a paint-brush and then what it looks like written in English letters. The original Japanese heading is at the top right. If you are going to send a message by radio you cannot use characters and so you have to use what the Japanese call 'kana'; these are fifty syllables, each of which has a morse equivalent, and they can be written down in English letters. Fu-ji-ya-ma represents four kana. These tell you how the Japanese sounds, but not which character is being used, and many characters have the same sound.

7

We worked every day from nine till five, and Saturday mornings, and every evening we had to learn a dozen or so new words and characters. We did not wear army uniform because our work was considered secret, and we stayed in private homes. A friend, Barry Smallman, and I lodged with Mrs Bottoms and her daughter, Vera, a large young lady who worked in a solicitor's office. We sometimes played cards with her, and one evening she persuaded us to take part in a séance. In a dim light we sat round a table with letters in a circle on it and an upturned glass. She said she was receiving messages through a medium from people who had died. We put our fingers on the glass with hers, and it moved from letter to letter spelling out words. We were not convinced and she got quite annoyed with us. I cannot remember the actual questions and answers because I was more concerned with the movements of the glass, but the general picture of life after death was incredibly dull, an existence remarkably like the one they had left. It did not sound at all like heaven to me; quite the reverse.

We even had to work on Christmas morning. I said to Chuu-i that I wanted to go to church. I was a confirmed member of the Church of England whose faith had been considerably strengthened by a group of Christians at Christ's, and I had no intention of allowing the army to stand in the way of my religious observance. He said, 'Fine. You go at eight o'clock and report here at nine.' On Boxing Day we went to a great party, and when I woke up the next day it was four o'clock in the afternoon and I felt very queer. I had 'flu and the doctor sent me home for a week to recover,

8

so I lost a few days' work. The course only lasted five and a half months, and the last two weeks were spent on code-breaking (or cryptography) because all Japanese army and naval messages were sent in code so that we should not be able to understand them if we picked them up on our radios.

Part of a Japanese code-book is shown overleaf. If they wanted to send a message containing 'air special wireless unit' (kookuu tokushu musentai), all they sent was '0700'. The person at the other end looked up the number in his book. We, of course, did not have the book (at least not normally) and so we had to break the code without it. How you do that is a complicated business which is touched on in Chapter 4. For your information 0670 means 'kookuu tsuushin shireibu' or 'air communications head-quarters'; each syllable represents one character.

The Bedford school was a remarkable, and very English, piece of improvisation. It was the invention of Colonel John Tiltman, an expert code-breaker who had been working at Bletchley Park, the home of government code-breaking since 1939, and had taught himself Japanese. After Pearl Harbour he was asked to recruit men who knew written Japanese and found about a dozen, mostly at the School of Oriental and African Studies in London. The School said it might be possible to train people in two years but not less. That was no good for Tiltman who was in a hurry, and he

9

turned to Captain Oswald Tuck, a retired naval officer who had studied Japanese in Japan on his own initiative and was eventually appointed Assistant to the Naval Attaché in Tokyo. On 21st December 1941 Tiltman asked Tuck to conduct the first six-months course for twenty-two men and one woman, most of whom were classical scholars from Oxford and Cambridge. Tuck, who had never taught anyone Japanese, commented in his diary 'the idea sounded impossible but was worth trying'. He tried, providing all the text books himself, five in number, and was brilliantly successful - at the age of sixty-five. Eric Ceadel was a student in that first class. Ours was the fifth.

We finished on the 9th February 1944 when we were told that twelve of us were going to be sent to Australia as quickly as possible because the need was urgent. Apparently Britain and America between them could find fewer than forty people who were competent in the language. My name was among the twelve. We were 'recalled to the colours' the next day, having been put on the Army Reserve, and had to go and do basic training to turn us into proper soldiers. But first we were allowed a few days' leave.

3973 航空教育隊
3782 航空地區司令部
0700 航空特殊無線隊
4698 航空特殊情報隊
9424 航空特殊通信隊
0670 航空通信司令部
3755 航空通信團
6829

10

CHAPTER 2

Wentworth Woodhouse

Thirteen of us went up to Yorkshire to a stately home called Wentworth Woodhouse which the army had taken over for training purposes. Alan Stripp was the thirteenth man, in reserve, and he did not finally go with us to Australia. It formed the depot for the Intelligence Corps which we joined, and we lived not in the big house, which was for officers only, but in the stables where we slept in double bunks. Behind my top bunk was a large brass ring for holding a horse's bridle, and every morning I had to polish it. Everything metal had to be polished and nearly everything else had to be whitewashed, including a pile of coal. Why? To teach us to obey orders without thinking.

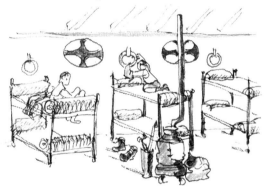

We were given our uniform and had to show ourselves to the sergeant-major. On seeing my very long great-coat (like a German army general's) he remarked, 'That's the nearest to a b----- general you'll ever get.' My friend Peter Hall did not like army ways and wore his hair long. 'Go and get your b----- hair cut', ordered the sergeant-major. He went to the army barber and reported back to the sergeant-major. 'I thought I told you to get yer 'air cut'. 'I've just been, sir', replied Peter. 'Well, go and b----- well get it cut again. Then come and show me.' So he went, and came back. 'I told yer to get it cut again.' 'Yes, sir. I've had it cut twice.' 'Well, go and b---- well get it cut again. Then come and show me.' So poor Peter had

11

to be shorn a third time before the sergeant-major was satisfied.

Our training was designed to make us fit. We had to drill every day, marching up and down the parade ground (square-bashing), and once a week do a route-march of eight or ten miles wearing full equipment and carrying a rifle. I got so hungry that I even enjoyed the rice pudding we were given when we got back. It was cold March weather and we had to wash and shave in cold water, though one of my duties was to heat a jug of water and take it to our officer. What I was looking forward to most was a fortnight's training on motor-bikes, but unfortunately that was cut out because they were in a hurry for us to finish. We had lots of dirty jobs to do, like sweeping and cleaning the main rooms in the big house. The officers who lived there did not use those rooms, and the furniture was covered with dust-sheets. One day a friend and I had to clean the drawing-room where we admired a fine Japanese painted screen. Its back was torn and I looked inside and found a lining of Japanese newspaper. I recognised some characters, but not enough to make much sense; the words we learned were nearly all military ones and did not figure in newspaper advertisements.

On the first Sunday morning I had permission to go down to the village church for the eight o'clock service. The Vicar was very friendly and invited me to breakfast. As Sunday was a day off, I accepted, and met his wife and two charming twin daughters, Monica and Angela. I thought they were sixteen, but Monica,

whom I met again recently, assured me they were thirteen. They did not go to school but had a governess for their lessons. They played the piano very well - and still do, now well into their sixties. We had a marvellous breakfast with bacon and eggs, the like of which we had not seen at home for years, but life in the country was different. We became good friends, and that, incidentally, is why our daughter is called Monica.

After six weeks of this rather grim life we were considered to be something like soldiers. They had intended that we should go on to an Officer Cadet Training Unit, but as we were wanted in a great hurry they decided to make us into warrant-officers straight away as the next best thing. So the day before we left the Depot we were promoted to company sergeant-major, and the expression on the face of our sergeant-instructor was a sight for sore eyes. We had to sew the badge on to the sleeves of our battle-dress blouses, and as most of us could not sew for nuts we trooped down to the Vicarage and kind Mrs Barnard sewed them on for us. The Intelligence Corps cap-badge was affectionately described as 'a pansy resting on its laurels'. (Which is presumably why, unlike most of the other Corps in the British Army, it has never been called Royal.) We were ready for the great journey half-way round the world.

We packed our kit-bags, which looked like fat sausages about a yard high, and travelled by train through the night to Scotland. The train was almost dark, with dim blue bulbs, and was full. We spent a very uncomfortable night in the corridor and did not sleep much. As soon as it was light I looked out of the window to see that we were arriving at Gourock on the river Clyde, near Glasgow, and there, proudly at anchor in the estuary, rode the world's largest passenger liner, the *Queen Mary*. The date was 2nd of April 1944.

CHAPTER 3

Half-way Round the World in Seventeen Days

The *Queen Mary* was so big that she brought across from America in one trip a whole division of soldiers, about 16,000 men, but going the other way, to America, she was nearly empty, with only a few hundred British airmen going there to train. We twelve were the only soldiers apart from a few Americans. The Americans counted warrant-officers as officers, so we ate in the officers' mess and slept in first-class cabins. Since the food was provided by the Americans it was unbelievably plentiful and good. The breakfast table groaned with eggs and bacon and butter and jam and coffee, all of which were strictly rationed in England. I could hardly get through it all.

We did actually work for our keep because each of us, with an American gunner, had to man one of the Bofors anti-aircraft guns placed on top of the huge ventilators towering above the top deck, some sixty or seventy feet above the grey waves. We were protected by a three-foot high fence, and the wind was bitter. Although we wore full woollen battle-dress with an overcoat and a duffle coat on top of that, after three hours up there I was so cold I could hardly climb down the ladder to the deck.

All other ships crossing the Atlantic went in convoy, guarded by destroyers to try to keep the German submarines away, but the *Queen Mary* was so fast (about thirty miles an hour) that no other ship could keep up with her. She sailed a zig-zag course so that submarines would find it difficult to aim torpedoes at her. At one point, on the third day, we saw a British plane, a Liberator I think, which circled around us and flashed a message with a signal lamp.

14

Not knowing the morse code I could not read it, but I gathered that we were being warned of U-boats lying in wait ahead, and so we turned north to get out of their way. Fortunately we did not meet any of them. That warning was almost certainly the result of a British intercept of a German naval *Enigma* message giving U-boat positions. In fact in that month, April 1944, the *Queen Mary* did meet a U-boat which fired three torpedoes at her, but they missed. She was travelling from west to east with 12,000 troops on board, and that was the only time when either of the *Queens* was attacked.

On the evening of the fifth day we arrived in New York. It looked magical, all lit up with no black-out. Car headlights shone (on the wrong side of the road) and the skyscrapers twinkled with all their lights on. We spent the night on board ship.

The next morning, April 7th, we boarded a train going west to San Francisco travelling in great comfort in Pullman coaches, with meals served by black waiters, a new experience for me. No one knew who we were or where we had come from. They did not recognise our uniform and found our accent very strange. They thought we might be Canadians or Australians, but could not believe that we were English. What were we doing travelling west? Michael Webster, who had a peculiar sense of humour, spread the rumour along the train that we were ski-troops from the Afghan Light Infantry. Half the Americans believed him.

Our longest stop, a whole afternoon, was at Chicago, the city famous for its gangsters. We did not see any, but did meet some kind ladies in a hospitality club who whisked us around the streets in high-powered cars at great speed. We travelled on through Omaha to the foot-hills of the Rocky Mountains where we stepped out of the train for an hour or two at Cheyenne, the home of Buffalo Bill. There was snow on the platform. Then on again for the last stage, across the Great Salt Lake to San Francisco - four days in all.

San Francisco, being on the Pacific coast, is famous in spring for its fog, and that is why we spent five days there seeing very little, not even the great Golden Gate bridge. Our camp was on a little island in San Francisco Bay, next to San Quentin, an island used as a convict prison. Each day we were taken to the airport by

15

boat and truck, but each day for four days it was fog-bound and so we had to come back. We spent a lot of time eating in American canteens where I discovered their habit of mixing all the courses together on one large dish (though per -haps that was only the army). For breakfast one would have bacon and egg and baked beans and tomatoes with waffles, all  swimming in maple syrup. Surprising what one can get used to!

The fifth day was fine enough for our Liberator to take off. The Lib. was really a large four-engined bomber with propellers, but a few had been converted for passenger-carrying over long distances. We were told that ours had recently been carrying Mr Churchill, our Prime Minister. First stop was Oahu, one of the Hawaian islands, a flight of well over 2,000 miles which took about seven hours. We arrived in the afternoon and it was baking hot. We went to the Post Exchange, the soldiers' club, and were greeted with jugs of iced pineapple-juice. We had not tasted that for years, and it was delicious.

A couple of hours for the plane to refuel and then we were off again, to Canton Island, one of the Phoenix Islands, just south of the Equator. That was the same distance again. It was dark when  we landed, after midnight, fortunately, because it was roasting hot and we were still wearing our winter woollies. We peeled them off layer by layer, but our shirts were thick wool and even our vests were woollen.

We took off again at four in the morning for Nanumea, a minute spot in the Ellice Islands, about 600 miles away. These islands are tiny coral atolls sticking up out of the deep blue Pacific ocean. A landing-strip had been bulldozed out of the coral,

16

MAP 1. ACROSS THE PACIFIC

dazzlingly white in the tropical sun. That, too, was hot. We took on board some crates of supplies. We had just crossed the Date Line where I lost one day out of my life, 19th April 1944. I need not have worried about that because I regained it many years later, in 1977, when I flew the Pacific the other way, from west to east, and so lived one day twice.

The next stage was over 1,000 miles to Guadalcanal in the Solomon Islands, just ten degrees south of the Equator. All I remember of this was sweaty heat, mud, battered palm trees, and very dejected-looking American soldiers. The Japanese had begun to construct an airstrip here in June 1942 and on 7th August 1942 the Americans landed to recapture the island. Fierce fighting lasted for nearly six months and many were killed on both sides. We were told that there were still a few Japanese hiding in the jungle up on the mountains in the centre of the island, but it was almost impossible to reach them.

I was glad to leave there, on the last lap to Brisbane on the east coast of Australia. I thought this was not far, but it turned out to be about 1,200 miles, a four hour flight. We arrived in the late evening of our second day, and were we tired! We were driven to an army camp and shown into a wooden hut which did not even have a bed. So we lay down on the floor and slept in our clothes with our kitbags for pillows. England to Australia, well over 12,000 miles, in seventeen days. The date was 20th April 1944.

CHAPTER 4

Brisbane

We got up next morning in a bit of a daze. Everything was strange. We thought a shower would be a good start, but when the Australian soldiers there saw us they roared with laughter. Most of them had been battle-hardened in the North African desert for a year or two and were burned dark brown. We had just come from an English winter and were lily white. They made some very rude comments.

One good thing was that we were soon issued with some tropical clothing: cotton khaki jackets, trousers and shorts, and also 'Jungle greens', blouses and trousers of dark green denim. We received army boots which were brown and not black and had no steel studs because these would soon rust in the tropics. To crown all we were issued with Australian slouch hats. We pinned up one side of them with the badge of the Australian Military Forces. Now we looked like Aussies, though we had yet to learn to speak Strine.

We were moved to our proper camp which consisted of small wooden huts on what had been Kedron Park race-course. We still had no beds, but at least had palliasses, straw mattresses, which softened the floor-boards a little. They positively encouraged hordes of insects of all sorts.

We were taken by lorry to work in another camp on another former race-course, appropriately named Ascot Park, again in wooden huts, but much larger and more comfortable ones. This was Central Bureau, a part of General MacArthur's General Head-quarters. We were a very mixed company including Americans, New Zealanders and South Africans as well as Australians, men and

19

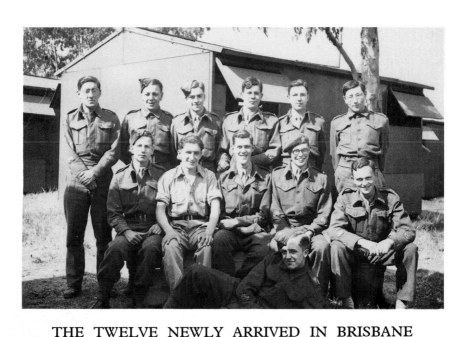

THE TWELVE NEWLY ARRIVED IN BRISBANE

Back Row left to right: Brian Warmington, Cyril James, Rupert Fenn, Michael Webster, Bernard Billingham, Bennie Polack
Seated left to right: Donald Fletcher, Peter Hall, Barry Smallman, John Smart, Hugh Melinsky. **In front:** Ray Eddolls

women, army, navy and air force. We twelve were split up, going to different sections. My section was 'Naval Air' (the Japanese did not have a separate Air Force, but their army and navy each controlled its own). Our task was to decode and translate messages picked up by Wireless Units which listened to Japanese aeroplanes, flying anywhere from Tokyo to Singapore, and to their bases, and sent the messages to us in Brisbane. These told us a great deal about what the Japanese were doing and were intending to do, and Captain Nave passed vital information immediately to the staff of General MacArthur who controlled all the American and Australian forces in the South-West Pacific Area.

Eric Nave was a short, slim man of forty-five, going grey and getting thin on top. Just after the First World War when he was a sub-lieutenant of twenty-one, having done very well in language examinations, he was sent off to Japan for two years to learn to speak and write Japanese fluently. He carried twenty-six gold

LT. ERIC NAVE, RAN, ACTING AS INTERPRETER
DURING THE VISIT OF THE JAPANESE NAVY TO
AUSTRALIA IN JANUARY 1924.
The photograph was taken on board the Japanese flagship *Asama*.
Seated from left to right: Engineer Lt. Cdr. Take Oka, Eric
Nave, Vice-Admiral Saito Sitichi Goro (later prime minister of
Japan), Engineer Captain Kishimoto.
Standing from left to right: Flag Lt. Shiraishi and
Cdr. Myoshi, staff officer.
(Photo: Eric Nave)

sovereigns in a belt round his waist for his pay and expenses. In the test at the end of this time he scored 91 marks out of 100. From that time on his job was to gather information from Japanese radio

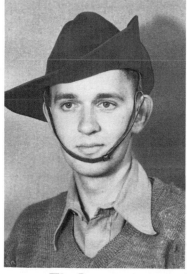

messages, and since much of it was in code, that code had to be broken. He taught himself how to do that. He was also, I believe, responsible for devising all the codes for the Royal Navy in the Pacific area.

What Captain Nave did not know about code-breaking was not worth knowing. He had a sixth sense which enabled him to sniff out a meaning in what looked to me like a jumble of letters or numbers. He gave me a collection of messages with some words already translated and told me to do the rest. I learned the hard way, for six weeks.

The Japanese approach to codes was quite unlike that of the Germans. Most of the important German messages for their three services used the *Enigma* machine, with variations, which was beginning to be broken at Bletchley Park from January 1940 onwards. The Germans were quite sure that it was unbreakable and unbroken, and remained so throughout the war. The Japanese, on the other hand, used a great variety of codes and cyphers. At any one time during the war at least fifty-five different systems were being used for army, navy, and diplomatic messages, of which twenty-four naval and twenty-one army have been identified. This is all the more remarkable considering their love of tidy organisation.

(There is a technical difference between a code and a cypher, though this is often blurred in many books: a code is a method of using groups of two or more letters or numbers to stand for words or phrases of a message; a cypher, or cipher to use the modern spelling, is a method of using letters or numbers to stand for the letters of a message, one at a time, or to change their order. All the work I did was with a code-book which used a four-kana

22

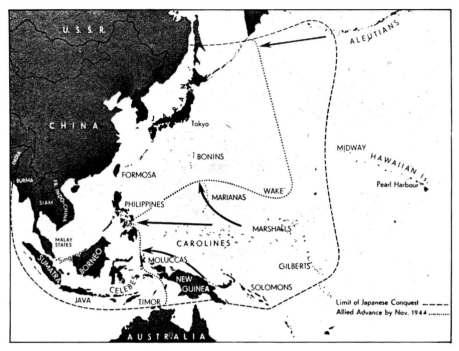

THE LIMITS OF JAPANESE CONQUEST

group to stand for a word or number, and a two-kana group to stand for a phrase, like 'estimated time of arrival'.)

Capt. Nave received messages from several wireless units. This was useful because if one version of a message contained gaps or faults another version might put these right. The greater the quantity of material available the better was the chance of breaking the code.

There were two great helps in this process. The first was being familiar with the shape of the message. Many messages were routine and followed the same pattern; for example, weather reports gave the place and time of origin, the general weather, the temperature, the amount of cloud, the wind direction and speed and perhaps the further outlook. In addition, the uncoded messages or 'traffic' from or to the aircraft might very well give a clue to one or several groups in a coded message.

23

The second were 'cribs', something which ought never to happen with well-trained wireless-operators. A plane is flying, say, to Balikpapan, and sends its estimated time of arrival. The base replies, 'Sorry we do not have your code-book 24; please send in 23.' The operator repeats the identical message in code 23, which the interceptors have already largely broken. So it is easy to read off all the groups in the new code 24. Code-books were changed regularly and it was not always easy to supply copies of the new books on time to the more distant outposts. In January 1943 two New Zealand corvettes rammed a Japanese submarine off Guadalcanal and forced it to beach on an outlying reef. It was found to be carrying 200,000 'code-books', (a word which may include other crypto materials), including, apparently, JN25, one of their most important naval codes. Much of this material was captured. The Japanese changed some of it but left JN25 unchanged.

Brisbane was not all work. We had one day off in seven (the unit worked a seven-day week), and I chose Sunday. People said that was stupid because there would be nothing to do then. How wrong they were! There was a club for servicemen where the lady in charge arranged for my friend Donald Fletcher and me to meet an Australian family at the cinema on a Saturday evening, and they took us home with them to spend the night. We slept on the verandah under mosquito nets. The next morning their two

daughters and son, about our age, took us for a long walk through the bush despite a temperature of ninety degrees. In the afternoon we went for a car ride to some beautiful spots and tasted strange fruit like avocado pears, custard apples and passion fruit. We turned up our noses at the common banana, but I did buy one for 3½d. In the evening we were joined by two American friends of theirs and had a grand party. The parents took us back to the camp rather late. It was all very different from Wentworth Woodhouse.

There were so many kind and hospitable families that I could have gone out almost every evening. They loved to hear about England, the bombing and the rationing, and they offered to send food parcels to our parents by post. Some of these actually arrived, months later. There were also concerts, a ballet, and dances, though army boots were unkind to one's partner's toes. I had to go and buy a pair of shoes, which were not rationed as in England, but I did not have long to wear them.

It seemed impossible to believe that a thousand miles away to the north, almost on the Equator, Australians and Americans were locked in a ferocious struggle with the Japanese in the most appalling conditions of jungle warfare. But so it was.

CHAPTER 5

The Wider Picture

We were thrown in at the deep end of Central Bureau's work, and it was only many years later that I learned about its background. It was set up by General MacArthur on 1st April 1942, a fortnight after he arrived in Australia (near Darwin) in a battered Boeing B.17 from the Philippines, and he made it the direct responsibility of Colonel, later Major General, S.B.Akin, his Chief Signals Officer. It was a joint American-Australian unit, its personnel being half American, a quarter Australian Army and a quarter Royal Australian Air Force, with other odd people like us who knew some Japanese. Its purpose was to gather information about the enemy from their radio signals, to decode and translate it, and prepare intelligence reports for MacArthur's staff.

One of the principal figures was Captain Eric Nave R.N., an Australian who had been based from 1937 to 1939 in Hong Kong, an admirable base for listening to Japanese broadcasts. In 1939 he moved to Singapore to the Far East Combined Bureau, and then to Melbourne in May 1940 to establish a Special Intelligence organisation for the Royal Australian Navy. In 1941 the Australian government authorised the training of Army and Air Force personnel for 'special intelligence', and the first group of seven R.A.A.F. and two Army skilled radio operators began their course in July of that year. One of the former was Clarrie Hermes whom I met at Darwin in 1944 with 2 Wireless Unit; he was known as 'The Immortal Sergeant' because he had been one ever since anyone could remember, and there was apparently no way in which he could be promoted while remaining a radio operator. In September 1941 they set off for Darwin, a journey which took them eleven days. They established themselves with much secrecy at the R.A.A.F. aerodrome there, and began work intercepting Japanese messages from Tokyo and their Pacific bases at Truk, Saipan, and Palau. At this time the R.A.A.F. began building its own intelligence group within the section at Melbourne.

Three months later the Japanese struck with devastating

THE WIDER PICTURE

strength, and without declaration of war, against the U.S. Pacific Fleet at Pearl Harbour, Hawaii. They launched 354 aircraft from six carriers which sank four battleships, sank or damaged fourteen other warships, and destroyed 188 American aircraft for the loss of 51 men. Fortunately the four American aircraft carriers were away on an exercise. The Americans were taken totally by surprise, which is amazing because Captain Nave himself had decoded Admiral Yamamoto's signal to proceed with the attack, and passed it to the highest authority, presumably Mr Churchill. At the same time the Japanese landed in Malaya and by mid-March had extended their grip almost to the eastern tip of New Guinea.

On 19th February 1942 the Japanese made a heavy attack on Darwin with 190 carrier-borne and 54 land-based bombers which flattened the town and devastated the aerodrome. The small intercept unit had been unable to give any warning and it was dispersed, but re-assembled the following month in Townsville, Queensland, where it became No.1 Wireless Unit on 25th April 1942.

That month the crisis deepened, with information received of enemy carriers moving to Truk and air reinforcements to Rabaul, indicating a coming attack on Port Moresby on the south side of New Guinea facing Australia. Intercepted intelligence knew of three carriers and five large cruisers, with a probable landing date between 8th and 10th May. The Americans strengthened their Task Force 17 with the carrier *Lexington*, and a bitter battle was fought in the Coral Sea (between New Guinea and Australia) from 4th to 8th May 1942 in which each side lost an aircraft carrier. But the Japanese retired and for the moment Australia was saved. Tokyo asked their New Guinea commander about a route across the island over the Owen Stanley mountain range to Port Moresby, and he replied that there was a rough track.

Admiral Yamamoto had one more grand plan, to capture Midway Island, drawing out the U.S.Navy from Honolulu and crushing it by overwhelming force. Fortunately his plans were known by intercept, and the Americans met the Japanese on 4th June 1942 and decisively defeated them, sinking four of their carriers along with 275 aircraft and their crews. Even then the Japanese still had the largest navy in the Pacific.

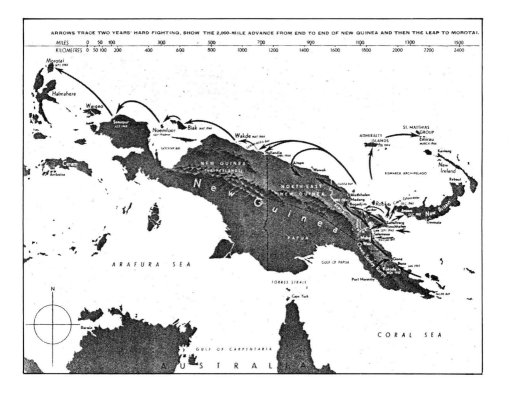

LEAPFROGGING UP THE COAST OF NEW GUINEA

In early June 1942 1.W.U. intercepted a message referring to the Japanese building an airstrip on an unknown island in the Solomons, spelled in kana GA DA RU KA NA RU. This turned out to be Guadalcanal. (The Japanese language has no 'L' sound because they cannot hear any difference between 'R' and 'L'.) The U.S. naval staff decided that it must be recaptured before the airstrip was completed, and so U.S. marines landed there on 7th August. A ferocious struggle continued until December with heavy losses on both sides. The allies lost four cruisers on 8th August partly because they were unable to decode a naval message about two Japanese cruiser divisions proceeding to Guadalcanal. The message was in JN 25 code which changed periodically and it took us time to catch up with the alterations.

The enemy was determined to press on in New Guinea/Papua and sent a powerful force of marines to capture Milne Bay at the extreme eastern end of the island. Central Bureau gained enough information to predict a landing at the end of August, and General MacArthur sent Australian reinforcements. The Japanese landed on 25th August, but after fierce fighting withdrew on 5th September, the first clear defeat of Japanese troops on land so far. Meanwhile they had been advancing over the mountains southwards toward Port Moresby. They were held by the Australians on the Kokoda Trail within sight of their objective in a savage battle under appalling conditions. By September 26th they were in retreat towards Buna where they had started. Their General Horii was drowned while crossing a flooded river.

The commander of the U.S. 5th Air Force, Lt. Gen. George Kenney, had become so dependent on the work of the Wireless Units that in December he asked the Australian government for five more, and a secret letter was sent to the Prime Minister, Mr Curtin. He approved of two immediately, one for Darwin and one for New Guinea. The former became 2 W.U. and the latter became the forward detachment of 1 W.U. which moved to Port Moresby on 8th January 1943. It took a long time to train wireless operators to the required standard and provide the special equipment necessary, but by the end of 1943 No. 2 W.U. (Naval Air) and No. 3 W.U. (Army Air) had been formed in Townsville.

By the beginning of 1943 the enemy, having withdrawn from

Papua and Guadalcanal, was determined to lose no more ground, and planned large reinforcements, some 6,500 men, for Lae on the north coast of New Guinea. The interceptors warned about the assembling of a large convoy with its destroyer escort near Rabaul, and on 28th February MacArthur's staff predicted a landing at Lae on 5th March. The U.S.Air Force and R.A.A.F. commanders were given the task of destroying this convoy on its way through the Bismarck Sea. It was sighted on the 2nd March, and over the next three days all eight transport ships and four of the eight escorting destroyers were sent to the bottom. Instead of the estimated 6,500 troops, only 850 were landed at Lae. Our forces lost six aircraft.

In the first half of April 1943 Yamamoto ordered large scale air attacks against Guadalcanal, Port Moresby and Milne Bay, and followed these up with a personal visit to his forward naval bases in the Bougainville-Solomons area. The Rabaul commander sent a message on the 13th giving the admiral's travel arrangements and this was picked up by 1 W.U. at Townsville, and also by the Americans in Honolulu. It was decoded almost entirely, and read:

'On 18th April C in C will visit RXZ [Ballale-Buin], R.. [?] and RXP in accordance with the following schedule:

Depart RR [Rabaul] at 0600 in medium attack plane escorted by 6 fighters.

Arrive RXZ at 0800. Proceed by minesweeper to R.. arriving at 0840.(Have minesweeper ready.) Depart R.. at 0945 and arrive RXZ at 1030.

Depart RXZ at 1100 in medium attack plane. Arrive at RXP at 1110.

Depart RXP at 1400 by medium attack plane and arrive RR 1540.

In case of bad weather the trip will be postponed one day.'

These bases were outside MacArthur's area and so the decision about attacking Yamamoto's plane was taken at the highest level in Washington. The argument would have gone something like this:

♦ Here's a golden opportunity to destroy our arch-enemy: remember he was personally responsible for Pearl Harbour. A squadron of P.38s from Henderson Field on Guadalcanal could just reach him - it's about 350 miles.

♦ Yes, but the Japanese would immediately suspect code-breaking because it is most unlikely that a squadron of P.38s would be patrolling there at the extreme limit of their range.

♦ But we can't let him go. He is the chief architect of their planning, and his death would be a great blow to their morale. It's worth the risk.

♦ If they think that we have broken their JN25 and introduce a new code to take its place we shall have lost one of our most valuable sources of information.

It was finally decided that he should be attacked in flight, and the decision was submitted to the President; he approved. On 15th April one of the wireless operators at 1 W.U. was interrogated by two U.S. officers about the top accuracy rating which he had given this message, but he was told nothing about its contents. He confirmed its accuracy.

On 18th April seventeen P. 38s took off from Henderson Field with extra fuel in belly-tanks and sighted their quarry at 0745 just off the southern tip of Bougainville, but were surprised to see *two* Betty bombers being escorted by the Zero fighters. After a brief battle with the Zeros, both bombers were shot down. Admiral Yamamoto's plane crashed in flames in the jungle and he was killed. The other, carrying Admiral Ugaki, his Chief of Staff, ditched in the sea, and he survived. Yamamoto's death was not announced by the Japanese until 21st May. The U.S. War Department said nothing. JN 25 was not changed. On 28th April Maj. Gen. Akin paid a special visit to 1 W.U. at Townsville and, on behalf of Gen. MacArthur, expressed their great satisfaction with the unit's operations.

On 16th August 1 W.U. reported a massive build-up of Japanese army bombers on Wewak, further west along the north coast of New Guinea, where there were four airstrips and something like 225 aircraft. Kenney threw everything he had against them from dawn on the 17th on through the 18th. The enemy lost 150 aircraft and over 300 mechanics. At the end of August they reported that there was no aviation fuel at Wewak or at Hollandia. On 3rd September 1 W.U. began operations in Port Moresby, and on 31st December 2 W.U. went into action at Darwin, followed there by 3 W.U. in March 1944.

By the autumn of 1943 the tide was turning. In September Lae and Salamaua were recaptured and in October Finschhafen also. 1944 began well for the code-breakers with a wonderful find at Sio, west of Sattelberg, of some steel boxes in a water-filled pit. These contained army high-grade code-books, which meant for

600 ム	630 受領(スス/スル)[受取(リ)]	660 (二)開設(スス)	680 命 令
601 サ イ	631 主トシテ	661 (ト)ナ リ/ルル ニ/ヤ	681 待 機(スス)
602 兵 團	632 信務班	662 符 號	682 右(方/側)
603 通命第○號	633 通信手	663 部 隊	683 指 示(スス)
604 不(可)能(ナ/ルル)	634 ラ シ ギ/ク	664 シ ム ベ キ/ム	684 (ノ)通 リ
605 西 北(方/側)	635 ニ モ	665 D (Г)	685 特(別)ニ
606 イ	636 器 材(字ム)	666 交 信(スス)	686 暗號書(字ム)
607 セント(スス/スル)	637 E (Д)	667 6.(六)	687 通信班
608 整 備(スス)	638 米(メートル)	668 開設豫定地	688 T (У)
609 目 的(字ム)	639 無 事	669 セ イ	689 訂(修)正(スス)
610 著 信	640 ベ ギ/ム	670 マ	690 不 明(ナ/ルル)
611 宛電報ナシ	641	671 ショク	691 明 瞭
612 ク ウ	642 第○聯隊	672 依賴(スス)[輻(ミ/ム)]	692 開所豫定時刻
613 經由(ニテ)	643 スウ(數)	673 對 所	693 ホ ウ
614 開 所	644 教 育(スス)	674 注 意(スス)	694 (ノ)指揮(下)(ニ/ヲ)
615 軍 隊	645 (二)屬(スス)	675	695 關係(上)
616 行・軍(シス/スル)	646 無線第○分隊	676 U (Ф)	696 小 隊
617 協 力(スス)	647 配 置	677 知ラセ	697 修 理
618 師團司令部	648 至 急	678 6	698
619 現在地(字ム)	649 要 旨	679 H (3)	699 再調査アリ度
620 ケン(件)	650 ス ベ ギ/ム		
621 通 過(スス)	651 自所名		
622 IO	652		
623 南(方/側)	653 シ スム/ムル		
624 ハ イ	654 シ タ リ/ヤ		
625 (ノ)管	655 約○料		
626 「 」	656 (シ)アラズヤ		
627 服 務(スス)	657 レ ン		
628 通信所	658 退 却(スス)		
629 トシテ	659 高射砲		

PORTION OF A JAPANESE CODE BOOK OF THE TYPE
CAPTURED AT SIO

the next two months instant translation of all main-line messages with top-level information.

During February the Japanese withdrew all their naval air forces from Rabaul and left 80,000 troops there to wither on the vine. They took to cultivating gardens since it was impossible to send them supplies. MacArthur's policy now was one of leap-frogging up the coast of New Guinea, cutting off pockets of the enemy (to be mopped up by the Australians) and establishing air bases ever nearer the Philippines. His next invasion was to be Hollandia, 500 miles westwards along the coast, whereas the Japanese were expecting it to be at Wewak. They were having to withdraw their main air bases westwards. Intercepts up to late March indicated that there were at least 310 aircraft parked on the Hollandia airfields, and on 29th March the interceptors picked up a message from the air commander, Lt. Gen. Teramoto, directing the Hollandia base commander to evacuate his planes the next morning. The message was quickly enciphered again and flashed down to Brisbane where, as it happened, Generals Akin and Kenney were attending a conference. It was taken by dispatch-rider to their hotel and received by Gen. Akin in his pyjamas, though he put his peaked cap on for the occasion. Having read the message through he took the lift up to Gen. Kenney's room and soon the order was on its way to Gen. Whitehead, the Air Commander in New Guinea, to attack Hollandia without delay. The next day, 150 planes struck at midday destroying 25 planes; on the following day 138 attacked and destroyed a further 138; and on 3rd April a third raid by 310

aircraft completed the destruction of what planes remained. Aerial photographs revealed 288 wrecked aircraft littering the runways. The way was paved for the invasion of Hollandia.

The wireless units, through Central Bureau, kept MacArthur's staff fully informed about the enemy's air plans, including sites of new airfields, movements of aircraft and their type, details of bombing and reconnaissance missions, fuel stocks, air cover over convoys, as well as weather reports. One valuable message of 3rd April reported that a flying-boat which departed Palau on 31st March was overdue at Davao in the Philippines. On board were Admiral Koga, Commander-in-Chief of the Combined Fleet (Adm. Yamamoto's successor) with half his staff. The plane had been forced down into the sea in an electrical storm. His death was not publicly announced until 8 May.

On April 20th 1944, General Whitehead, commanding the U.S. 5th Air Force, sent a message to the Commanding Officer of 1 W.U. 'to express appreciation and to register commendation for the superior work which you and the men under your command are doing...'.

On the same day the allied convoy of over 200 ships set off from the Admiralty Islands northwards (to deceive the enemy), then turned west, and finally south, hitting the beaches at Hollandia the next morning. The Japanese were taken totally by surprise. Gen. MacArthur went ashore four hours after the landing and was well satisfied. Three thousand Japanese had perished at the cost of 300 American casualties, and a further 30,000 of the enemy had been cut off and isolated from any effective action.

A month later a similar scene was enacted at the island of Biak, another 300 miles to the west, and by June 22 the Americans had captured three airstrips. The invasion of the Philippines was now imminent and Gen. Akin wanted the R.A.A.F. Wireless Units to cover the convoy and the first landing, the only non-American personnel. Special permission was given: 'R.A.A.F. components of G.H.Q. units will be available for service anywhere, at the discretion of G.H.Q.'.

Round the other side of the world, D-day had taken place on 6th June, 1944, and allied troops were fighting fiercely in Normandy for the liberation of Europe.

CHAPTER 6

Darwin

In the middle of June 1944, six weeks after arriving at Brisbane, I was posted to No. 2 Wireless Unit, Royal Australian Air Force, in, or rather near, Darwin, 1600 miles away on the north coast of Australia. It is such a huge country that no one notices these vast distances. I flew it in a day in a Dakota, a gallant work-horse but not one designed for passenger comfort. There were no proper seats but only canvas benches along the sides of the fuselage and no seat-belts, with crates on the floor. After several hours, flying became distinctly bumpy and the sky darkened. We were soon enveloped in clouds and could see nothing else outside the windows except vivid flashes of lightning. Suddenly the plane would drop fifty feet, leaving one's stomach behind. Then it would be thrown a hundred feet up and one's stomach went through the seat. After a quarter of an hour of this I was past caring. I have never been more grateful to step down on to firm ground again.

My arrival did not work out well. My unit was sixty miles from Darwin, in the bush at Coomallie Creek. An airman had been sent to meet me and take me there, but we failed to make contact and so I set off hitch-hiking. No one knew where the unit was (and neither did I), but late in the evening I managed to telephone them. An officer came to collect me in a lorry and delivered me after midnight. He showed me to my tent and I slept well.

We were woken at seven by loudspeakers, 'The Voice of Coomallie', with music and news (often with Big Ben from London); we washed and shaved in cold water in the open air - and so to breakfast. There was a combined officers' and sergeants' mess of about twenty; the airmen ate and slept in another part of the camp. The unit was about sixty all told.They received me politely but were somewhat puzzled by this strange young Pommie who had dropped in from nowhere.

The operational part of the unit was at the top of a hill and consisted of three large lorries with a canvas awning stretched between two of them. Under this I and four or five others worked at tables, with the wireless sets in one lorry and the Intelligence Officer in the other. The third lorry contained generators for providing the electricity. (Electric light was plentiful up at 'ops' but

elsewhere in the camp it was severely rationed. We had it in the messes but not in our tents.) Airmen brought me messages which the operators had picked up listening to Japanese aeroplanes, and I did my best to decode and translate them. The other 'traffic' consisted of all the other signals sent out by the planes and their bases, and this was carefully examined and collected.

We had a teletype line to Brisbane (which was like a typewriter on a telephone line) and every message we received was sent down to Capt. Nave. This land-line was not 'secure' since anyone could tap into it, and so every one of our messages had to be enciphered by our unit and then deciphered at Central Bureau. After I had been on the unit several months I discovered that the machine we used for this, a Typex, had been made by a firm in Croydon in a factory which I passed every day on my way to school. I had to go half way round the world to find out what they made there!

Life was very busy when I arrived, with over a hundred messages a day. I started work at eight in the morning, had breaks for lunch and tea (what we should call supper) and then went back till nine or ten at night. I had a corporal to help me and later two airmen as well. I did not have a day off for three and a half months. The commonest messages were weather reports which were valuable to us for preparing weather forecasts. The most exciting messages were those from and to aeroplanes escorting convoys and giving their positions. These were anywhere between Japan and the Philippines, or New Guinea or Singapore, or Java or Sumatra or the other islands of the Dutch East Indies. These went straight to Capt. Nave and if he could work out the position he would telephone the American naval staff who would send a wireless message to the nearest allied submarine to attack the convoy with torpedoes.

In February 1944 in the closing days of Rabaul's importance (just before I arrived in Darwin) 1 W.U. and 2 W.U. began intercepting positions of convoys; these were coming down from the north, and positions were given either by escorting aircraft reporting back to base, or by the base giving a position to aircraft so that it or they could find the convoy. Here is a typical actual message, with translation, though it uses three-kana groups whereas I worked with 4-kana groups:

SE	NO	SU	sendan	convoy
ME	U	TE	no	of
MU	KU	NO	ichi	position
TU	RO	HI	R	Rabaul
YA	U	TI	kichi	base
TO	MO	TI	32	32
TU	RI	NE	6	6
MO	SI	HE	50	50
YA	SU	KE	shinro	course
MU	KA	NU	355	355
TI	HO	SO	sokuryoku	speed
YA	HO	NA	8	8

Translation: Position of convoy: bearing 326 degrees, 50 miles, from Rabaul base; course 355 degrees, speed 8 knots.

Many successful sinkings were achieved in the second half of 1944, especially with those convoys plying from Japan to Singapore via Manila, and picking up vital oil from Borneo on the return trip. So valuable was this fuel that the Japanese even used battleships to escort their tankers.

Each word in our messages was made up of four kana syllables, like KO FU TE SI which might stand for 'enemy', together with some two syllable groups, like HI TO which might stand for 'expected time of arrival is...' Every evening I sent to Capt. Nave a list of groups which I thought I had broken together with their meanings, and every morning I received back from him a list confirming them if they were right, correcting them if they were wrong, and giving me additional ones. Sometimes we had long arguments about the meaning of a group; one lasted for three days, at the end of which it was clear that I was right, and he surrendered. (Soon after that I heard that I had been recommended for a commission.)

Just to make matters worse the Japanese changed this particular code-book about every twelve days, but our wireless operators were very canny. The most experienced of them, like Sergeant Clarrie Hermes, knew the touch of the Japanese operators so well that they could tell which plane was transmitting even if it had just changed its call-sign. Before I arrived he had also been doing the translating, and he was entirely self-taught. I felt rather mean taking it away from him. After I had been there three months I was sent an actual code-book which had been captured (I suppose from a crashed plane), and I spent a lot of my 'spare' time translating it into English. It gave one more of the feel of a Japanese message when one was familiar with the book from which it came.

It was hot work. We only ever wore 'shirt-sleeve order' and generally did not bother with shirts except after dark when the mosquitoes attacked. I even stopped wearing socks and found Australian boots with their supple leather quite comfortable. The temperature was usually over eighty degrees, with little difference between winter and summer. There was a dry season from February to November and the rest was wet, so wet that you could pretty well see the grass growing - it grew five feet in a month. When I arrived the weather was dry with clear blue skies for weeks on end until one

IN THE BUSH, DARWIN

yearned for a good English fog. The nights were cooler and one might need a blanket in bed. A mosquito net was always necessary. We had to shower after sundown because the water-pipe up from the creek became so hot on the hillside that it nearly boiled the water. When you drank a mug of hot tea you could feel a trickle of perspiration down your spine, but you thought that you felt relatively cool afterwards.

The heat and constant perspiration produced a lot of skin troubles, about which the Medical Officer did not seem to know a great deal, or maybe the remedies did not then exist. His favourite treatment was a dye called gentian violet, and some men looked pretty weird walking around with large purple patches painted on them.

The ground was dry and stony, but the gum-trees, or eucalyptus, kept their leaves all the year. Ants crawled everywhere, and the white ants ate nearly everything. I had to build a cupboard on legs and stand the legs in tins of water to stop the ants eating my boots. There were ant-hills everywhere up to ten or twelve feet high.

THE SHOWERS, DARWIN

There were also snakes. Some were poisonous like the adders, but others were not, like the rock pythons, though you did not want to get one round your neck. One of the airmen found a twelve-foot specimen on his bed; he shot  it and hung it from a rafter in the roof of the officers' mess when they had gone down the road to an open-air cinema show. Later the evening darkness was pierced by a fearsome scream. One of the officers had walked straight into the hanging snake.

There were also goannas, lizards three or four feet long, which shinned up trees with great agility and were harmless. Sometimes we saw a flash of red and green and black as a parrot flew by. Kangaroos were quite tame and came thudding through the camp, sometimes with a baby in the front pocket.

The food was not exciting, most of it either coming out of tins or reconstituted after dehydration. Our Commanding Officer was not very fair as he told the cook to serve most of the fresh meat (steak) to the officers, while the men had 'M&V' (tinned meat with vegetables). The men got fed up with this and decided to go on strike. Suddenly they were unable to hear any Japanese aircraft! So no messages went down to Brisbane. The C.O. punished the culprits by making them build a road, but after a few days a wing-commander flew up from Brisbane, and that C.O. was removed. Then the messages started to flow again, and the men received their fair share of the steak.

41

One of my best friends was Sgt Rollie May who in peacetime was a concert pianist in Adelaide. We had an old piano in the
mess which had several keys missing
and used to have beer poured down
it during parties. I got him to play
some Beethoven on it (from the
Appassionata Sonata),but he
could not bear it. We went to
several concerts either of recorded
music or occasionally of live. Several
thousand people flocked to an
open-air recital by a famous
opera singer, Marjorie Lawrence,
with some of the audience hanging
from palmtrees.

We had one dance in the mess when a load of A.W.A.S.
(Australian Women's Army Service) was delivered by lorry, in
uniform. The rule was 'no alcohol', but we all drank buckets of
'jungle juice' into which more than one bottle of gin had been
poured. Some of us received a return invitation and travelled a mere
forty miles to their camp. That dance was better because they were
allowed to wear civilian dress.

THE OFFICERS' & SERGEANTS' MESS, NO.2 W.U., CHRISTMAS DAY 1944 -
WITH THE COOK

On Christmas Day, one of the hottest of the year, I had to eat two hot Christmas dinners. The officers had theirs at midday, of turkey and Christmas pudding, served by the men. Then in the evening the men had theirs, of roast beef and Yorkshire pudding, served by the officers, and we ate the same afterwards.

CHAPTER 7

The Battle for the Philippines

The pace of the allied advance had been so swift that the date for the invasion of the Philippines, the last step before Japan itself, was brought forward to 20th October 1944, and the place was to be Leyte, an island in the centre. By order of General MacArthur a detachment of 24 wireless operators and intelligence personnel was withdrawn from 1 W.U. at Biak and flown to Hollandia to join the huge American invasion force, under the personal care of General Akin. A further 94 personnel, some from 1 W.U. and some from 6 W.U. (a new unit forming in Brisbane) followed soon after, going ashore on November 5th.

In the convoy Gen. Akin took five of the Australians and one Englishman, Peter Hall, on his own communications vessel PCEV 848, the rest being embarked on a tank-landing ship. The task of the six was to keep a full-time watch on all the Japanese bomber, fighter, and base frequencies during the six or seven days required for the convoy to reach Leyte. On the water were five top U.S. generals with their headquarters staffs.

At dawn on 17th October, when the convoy was about 200 miles south of Leyte, a lone enemy reconnaissance aircraft sighted it. The Japanese radio operator went berserk, overawed by the immensity of the armada, and could hardly tap out his message in plain language. There were, however, few air attacks because the Japanese air force was fully engaged with a force of U.S. aircraft-carriers. Our interceptors provided a running commentary on enemy preparations until, at dawn on the 20th October, the invasion began with a thunderous naval bombardment, watched by Gen. Akin and his Australians with Peter Hall. The following morning the six landed at Tacloban and pitched their tents in the U.S. headquarters camp. It was a hair-raising night during which a bomb landed on the ship they had just left, killing sixty of the crew. War correspondents were most surprised to find Australian slouch hats amid the American forces and dubbed the group 'The Foreign Legion'.

The Japanese launched the entire might of their fleet against the invading ships, including the two largest battleships in the world, the *Yamato* and the *Musashi*, and from 22nd to 24th October the biggest naval battle in history was fought, the Battle of Leyte Gulf, which very nearly spelt disaster for the Americans. At the critical moment, however, Admiral Kurita turned back and victory was assured. Two hundred and eighty-two ships took part, and the Japanese lost four aircraft-carriers, three battleships, six heavy cruisers, three light cruisers and three destroyers; the Americans lost three small carriers and three destroyers. It was the end of the Japanese navy.

On land the enemy fought fiercely, relying on heavy air attacks from the huge Clark Field in Luzon, the northern island. Their signals were so loud that our operators could dangle their earphones round their necks and still hear then clearly. The critical messages concerned the Japanese troop transport convoys bringing desperately needed reinforcements into the port of Ormoc. These had to be escorted by aircraft which obligingly gave full information of the ships' movements and particularly their estimated time of arrival. American aircraft were alerted and gave them a warm reception. On 11th November an entire troop-laden convoy was destroyed. Altogether 6 W.U. was credited by the air force authorities with the destruction of seventeen ships.

The only day when 6 W.U. was off the air was 30th October when their camp was almost obliterated by a typhoon with winds of a hundred miles an hour and torrential rain. The site was reduced to a sea of mud, and in the forty days after landing thirty-four inches of rain fell.

By Christmas 1944 the Leyte campaign was virtually completed. General MacArthur had landed 200,000 troops there and Gen. Yamashita had lost 65,000 of his best men. Gen. Akin wrote: 'Worthy of official mention was the landing at Leyte (with the first troops to land) of an Australian intercept detachment...Its prompt action there provided early intercepts that were invaluable.'

Realising that their plight was desperate, the Japanese resorted to a new and sinister weapon, the suicide bomber or *kamikaze*. The name means 'divine wind', a reference to a fierce gale which swamped the invading boats of Kublai Khan seven hundred years before. On 25th October at 0740 a piloted missile plummeted out of a cloud on to the flight deck of the aircraft-carrier *Santee* and on through the hangar deck before exploding to start a raging fire. Despite a subsequent torpedo the ship was saved. Three hours later five Zeros, each with a 500lb. bomb, attacked the carriers again, and the fifth hit the flight deck of the *St Lo* and plunged through to start an enormous fire and a series of explosions. In less than half an hour the ship had sunk. Admiral Toyoda, the Commander-in-Chief of the Combined Fleet, sent a message to the Japanese Naval Air Command reporting this successful attack and giving the names of the aircrew who had sacrificed their lives.

An intercept of 3rd November disclosed the formation of a 'special attack unit' at Clark Field of twenty-two bombers and fighters, the first to be devoted to suicide bombing. Other similar units soon followed, with no apparent shortage of volunteers. No. 6 W.U. discovered their radio frequencies and plotted their flight pattern from the homeland through Formosa (now Taiwan) into Clark and Nichols Fields in the late evening in order to fly out again early in the morning. The air and naval headquarters were duly alerted and aircraft were dispatched before dawn to destroy them. The *kamikaze* scheme proved to be the greatest single threat for the Americans until the end of the war.

General MacArthur did not delay. On 2nd January 1945 a massive invasion force of over a thousand ships set off for Lingayen, in Luzon, the main northern island of the Philippines. Again Gen. Akin picked Wireless Unit personnel to accompany him although he had the choice of several American intercept units. The landing was successful despite several *kamikaze* attacks. The detachment with Gen. Akin was joined later on in Luzon by the remainder of 6 W.U. from Leyte, by the newly-formed 5 W.U. from Brisbane and some members of 4 W.U. from Hollandia. They formed a unique 'foreign' presence, with some Britishers, in the Philippines.

On 27th January 1945 the Americans captured Clark Field and found over six hundred wrecked Japanese aircraft strewn round the edges of its six airstrips. American firepower was invincible and their troops reached the outskirts of Manila on 3rd February. The Japanese army had pulled out, but the naval commander used his 16,000 men to contest every inch. The city was terribly damaged, and 100,000 Filipino citizens were killed before the city was finally liberated on 3rd March.

CHAPTER 8

A Month in Sydney

After eight months in Darwin I had had enough, particularly with the wet season in full flood. I had not been in too good health, with a touch of bronchitis, and the poor food did not help. Escape came in an unusual way. The Australian government had sent a notice inviting men to apply to join the Australian Diplomatic Service after the war, to represent that government abroad. I thought I would have a go, though I did not know too much about Australia, and sat an examination on the unit on September 2nd. Weeks later I was told to come for an interview in Sydney in January. So that got me out of Darwin, just after my twenty-first birthday which was on January 25th, 1945. I celebrated it with a food parcel from Brisbane, and a piece of music (Beethoven I think) played for me on the B.B.C. 'Forces Favourites' programme. Odd, hearing one's name relayed half way round the world!

A flight was arranged from Darwin, but the transport people made a complete mess of it so we had to stop half way and spend the night at Cloncurry which is in the middle of nowhere. The town looked just like one in a Western cowboy film, and the hotel in which I stayed was a wooden one with a post in front for the tethering of one's horse. I ordered a plateful of poached eggs, washed down with a huge milk-shake with a dollop of ice-cream on top because we had tasted neither eggs nor fresh milk for eight months, nor fresh fruit or vegetables. The joy of sleeping in clean, ironed, white sheets!

We arrived in Brisbane the next day, the 31st, with no onward plane available. So I went back to Central Bureau and was glad to meet old friends again. The Commanding Officer, Colonel Sandford, was sympathetic and kindly gave me a bed for the night in his own house. The next day I was advised to go on to Sydney by train, which turned out to be a journey of twenty-four hours with no bed; I tried to sleep sitting up, not very successfully. By now I was feeling a bit of a wreck. I arrived after lunch and found my interview was at half past four that afternoon. I could not even have a shower, but managed to pull out a clean but unironed shirt from my kit-bag. I was only two days late, but by then I was past caring.

I was shown in for my interview and sat down facing five distinguished-looking men who fired questions at me. Where had I been educated? What did I know of Greek and Latin and Greece and Rome? (Not much by then.) What was I doing in the army? How had I learned Japanese? Where did my name come from? (From Russia where my grandfather was born and lived as a boy.) I made them laugh by saying that I had started reading 'Paradise Lost' in Darwin. In the end I did not get the job, but I started a wonderful month's leave in Sydney.

My recollections of that interlude are a little hazy, partly because I was not feeling terribly well, but I have some letters written home at the time which supply some colourful details. I remember a mad round of wonderfully generous entertainment in all sorts of homes with people who were quite unknown but welcomed me like a long-lost son.

It started with Mr Salmon who was the brother-in-law of an officer in Darwin. I rang him up and he invited me out to his home in Croydon (a strange coincidence since that was the name of my home-town), apologising that his wife was away. We went round to friends, the Knights, for meals and I had the freedom of both homes with meals thrown in as required. They both had sons serving in the Royal Australian Air Force in England and were only too glad to have me in return. One day we had a picnic on one of Sydney's famous beaches and this is what we took: a loaf, half a pound of butter, a tin of tongue and a tin of luncheon meat, lettuce, tomatoes, tea, milk, apple pies, a fresh pineapple, half a pint of cream, and a huge cake. I wrote to my parents: 'I shall soon know Sydney far better than I know London, and in a month here I shall have got to know many more people than I did in fifteen years at home'.

A Red Cross nurse, a friend of Mr Salmon's, invited me to a magnificent army hospital to visit a young man who had broken his back and would probably spend the rest of his life in hospital. He had been a stockman in charge of cattle up north, and we talked about the Northern Territory where Darwin is. I also met the wife of a sergeant in my Darwin unit whose father came from England,

and they invited me to spend a day with them. They all wanted desperately to hear about the 'home country' and particularly about the bombing, the 'doodle-bugs' (flying bombs which I had not experienced) and the rationing of food and clothes.

One day I got myself invited out to lunch with the Professor of Greek at Sydney University with a couple of other professors who were all Cambridge men, and we had a good talk about...guess what? I was shown over the University and then taken to a Chinese meal. I managed a game of golf one afternoon and an evening's tennis at the home of one Mr Vernon. One Sunday I spent at the home of a bachelor who seemed to be wedded to his grand piano which he played very well. He also had a fine collection of records.

Towards the end of my twenty-four days I met a charming young lady, Innes Murdoch by name, who was a ballerina and had danced with modern European ballet before the war. She was working with the Free French Society there - a curious mix-up. We went to a ballet and talked a great deal about England. Made me quite homesick.

WITH INNES IN SYDNEY

It was now time for me to go back to Brisbane, but the transport officer told me, with a wink in his eye, that there would be no seat on the train for a couple of days, so I had better take some more leave. I phoned up a Mr Barker whom I had met in Brisbane Toc H (a servicemen's club) eleven months before when he gave me his card. He remembered me and invited me to stay, and I had the pleasure of meeting his wife and two charming daughters, Alison and Beatrice, both about my age. We got on very well; it was only a pity that I had left it so late. I remember reading to Beatrice some of Eliot's 'Four Quartets', only recently published, which I had bought in Sydney, but she did not understand much of it. I am not sure that I did either, but it made a change.

I managed to wangle another day or two's leave and finally was put on a train on 3rd March. As I was the only other (warrant) officer, I was made Adjutant to the Commanding Officer, a pleasant Australian major, and thus had a comfortable bed for the night on the train. Twenty-four hours later we steamed into Brisbane and soon I was back with my friends. There were also six new Pommies who had just arrived as a second group from England. After Darwin, Brisbane would have been a paradise. But Sydney had spoiled me.

A FLYING BOMB ('DOODLEBUG')

CHAPTER 9

Back in Brisbane

Actually I had a pleasant six weeks back in Brisbane. At first it was terribly hot, February being midsummer in those parts. Soon after I arrived, at the beginning of March 1945, I spent the hottest night of my life with a temperature of 79 degrees and a humidity of 96 per cent. No wonder I woke up in a pool of water. After that it gradually cooled off until the weather was like a hot English summer. It was quite usual to go to a dance in shorts and a shirt.

A pile of letters awaited my arrival, including a detailed account of my elder sister Joan's wedding with Roger Hughes, which had taken place on 24th February at St Mary's Church, Addiscombe. (The invitation reached me on the 20th April.) I was telling an A.W.A.S. officer in my section about this, and of course the first question she asked was 'What was she wearing?' That was one detail which my mother had not described. Later I discovered she wore a navy blue suit; it was impossible to make a white wedding dress because of the clothes' rationing.

I went back to work with Capt. Nave, only this time I worked in shifts, one week from nine till five, the next week from four in the afternoon till midnight. There was one big change: on 26th March my commission arrived and I became Lieutenant Melinsky. (The Intelligence Corps did not bother with Second Lieutenants.) I had to get used quickly to being saluted rather than saluting. It was lovely being woken at half-past six by my batman (servant) and lying in bed reading the Courier Mail while he polished my shoes for me. Unfortunately that did not last long.

I had known for some time that I was going to be commissioned and when I was in Sydney I bought a Sam Browne leather belt and polished it up well. I thought my parents would like a picture of me all dressed up, and so I borrowed another English officer's service dress which happened to fit, put on my belt and the cap I had brought with me from England, and had myself photographed. No one else ever saw me looking like that in Australia.

Five of us were commissioned including Peter Hall who had been with No. 1 W.U. in New Guinea and was now on Leyte in the Philippines. I had the distinct impression that some of our twelve had been in Melbourne engaged on the translation of inter-cepted diplomatic messages. Whether that was so or not, it is certainly true that some of the most valuable information the allies gained about Germany and the defences of northern Europe came from the messages sent to Tokyo from Berlin by members of the Japanese Embassy there. At the beginning of May 1944, for example, the Japanese Naval Attaché in Berlin was taken on a tour of coastal defences in northern France, and in three messages to Tokyo described in detail German operational policy and their main units, coastal batteries and other defences, the effect of allied air raids, expectations about allied landings and the state of German morale. On 24th April 1944 Vice-Admiral Abe, the head of the Japanese Naval Mission in Berlin, and the Attaché, visited Admiral Doenitz who gave them the latest information about two new types of U-boats being developed. This was followed by a visit on 29th August to inspect production of the new Type XXI U-boat. All this was duly reported with typical Japanese thoroughness, followed later by full details of the boat's construction, performance and planned output.

But back to Brisbane. When we first arrived there its citizens thought we were the vanguard of the British Army. They soon discovered that we were not, and when they had got over their disappointment, they gave us their undivided attention. The Hooper family in particular adopted us Pommies, and Mrs Hooper gave us the run of her large house, with meals or a bed for the asking. She had two sons, one of whom had been killed at Rabaul, and three daughters, two of whom were married; the third, Bette, was still at home and about to celebrate her eighteenth birthday. We went to her party. Some party!

They also had a seaside house at Southport. I spent a delightful Easter with friends of theirs at Surfers' Paradise nearby, a vast beach of silver sand on which the Pacific surf creamed in with a steady roar. It was lovely to walk along by moonlight: there was hardly another house in sight. (Today it is built up solid.) Early in the morning, before breakfast, their son, an air force pilot, woke me up for a bathe in the surf. I had never been in it before. He told me about 'dumpers', ten-foot high waves which pick you up and then dump you down under the surface, but he had not told me about the undertow which pulls you backwards out to sea, still under the water. I was duly dumped and pulled back and found it very hard to get up to the surface. It was quite frightening. I enjoyed my breakfast afterwards. For lunch we had oysters and crab, pineapple and bananas, with several other delicacies thrown in. And of course iced beer.

In the middle of April, as I had expected, I received orders to pack my kit-bag and prepare to move north again. (For this journey you will need to look at the map on p.55) The worst part of the preparation was receiving four inoculations, one after the

53

other against typhus, tetanus, smallpox and cholera, as we trooped round in a large circle, all in one afternoon outdoors in the blazing sun. I managed a dinner-party that evening; fortunately the next day was my stand-down, or day off.

TRAVELS IN THE SOUTH WEST PACIFIC

CHAPTER 10

Westwards to Borneo

By this time, April 1945, the war in Europe was nearly finished; gigantic British and American armies were sweeping into Germany from the west, and Russian ones from the east. It was only a matter of time before they would meet, and that would be the end of Hitler. But things were quite different for us. The Americans had recaptured most of the Philippine Islands and were preparing for the final attack on Japan itself. The Australians were pressing westwards towards Malaya and Singapore. The Japanese would fight to the last man.

On the way to Singapore from New Guinea is the large island of Borneo, vital to the Japanese as a rich source of oil. I was to take part in a sea-borne invasion of part of the island with a detachment of No. 4 Wireless Unit. (The other part of the Unit was going to Balikpapan on the east coast of Borneo.) On the evening of 13th April I left by plane on a long journey. First stop was Townsville at three o'clock in the morning of the 14th for re-fuelling; then on to Finschhafen on the north coast of New Guinea where we arrived at a quarter past four in the afternoon. I had to wait three days for an onward flight, and that was my introduction to life on a tropical island, consisting mainly of green tents, palm trees, heat and mud.

On 17th April I left Biak at twenty past eight in the morning and arrived at Morotai at midday. This is a little island half way between New Guinea and the Philippines which the Americans had reoccupied the previous September with its two valuable airfields. In November-December the Japanese made a rather feeble effort to regain it, but it came to nothing. There were still some Japanese soldiers on the island but they did not bother us or stop the allies from using the island as a major air and naval base. No. 4 W. U.'s first camp-site was a piece of jungle flattened by bulldozers about half a mile from the sea. A little later we moved to a much pleasanter place next to the beach among palm trees with their coconuts. There was little work to do because we were still getting

56

ready. Tony Carson and I were two Army officers in an Air Force unit and so we spent some time trying to turn the airmen into fighting troops just in case we should meet some Japanese. I do not know whether we were successful because fortunately the matter was not put to the test.

We spent most of our time, however, either spine-bashing (a picturesque Aussie term for resting on our beds) or bathing in the beautifully warm sea where one could spend an hour without getting cold. There were coral snakes which one had to watch out for because they were deadly. We also had an assortment of boats: a large rubber raft, a canoe made from an aeroplane's belly tank, and a dinghy, and down the road was a Yankee unit owning a yacht with whom we made friends. For reading matter I had brought with me *Pickwick Papers*, and by the time we left Morotai I had read five hundred pages. In the evening we went down the road to an outdoor cinema which I once visited four nights running. It was strange watching English films under a tropical moon. The weather was hot and sometimes very wet, so much so that we had to dig trenches round our tents.

On 10th May the war in Europe finished. Mr Churchill, the Prime Minister, made his historic statement on the radio at ten o'clock in the evening our time, and the boys gathered round to hear him. But the King's broadcast was not until four o'clock in the morning, and so Tony and I and one or two others took a radio down to the beach, together with our beds, and we followed the B.B.C.'s tour round Britain, to Liverpool, Cardiff, Edinburgh and

PALMS
ON MOROTAI

MOROTAI BEACH FROM THE PIER

Belfast, heard the crowd outside Buckingham Palace cheering tumultuously, and then finally listened to the King speaking. It was strange, lying beneath the Southern Cross with the Pacific lapping by our side.

Finally, on 1st June, we embarked on our ship with lorries, tents and equipment. There were, I was told, about 200 ships carrying between them two-thirds of the Australian Ninth Division, about 8,000 men. There were landing ships to carry the soldiers and tanks to the beach, and there were cruisers and destroyers to protect the convoy. Our voyage lasted ten days; it was peaceful and enjoyable. The crew of our ship gave up their bunks for us officers to sleep in; the men had to sleep on deck where they could amid all the lorries and equipment. By day we played bridge or listened to records or just gazed over the side. One evening the sea around us was lit up with shoals of shimmering silver fish. Once we had rounded the northern tip of Borneo we kept within sight of the coast and soon saw the splendid 12,000-foot peak of Mount Kinabulu.

We got up early in the morning of 10th June and found that we had arrived. The whole convoy had anchored by the island of Labuan, off the north-west of Borneo. All was quiet. As I stood on the deck in the half light of a clear dawn I saw a dark spot in the sky diving down followed by a great fountain of water near a neighbouring ship. Only then did I realise what it was, and suddenly every anti-aircraft gun opened up; but the plane was gone. That was all we saw of the Japanese Air Force.

At precisely eight o'clock the morning calm was shattered as every warship opened up with its big guns firing on to the Japanese coastal defences. The peaceful shore beneath its swaying palms shook and leapt, and dark columns of dirt rose and fell, to be replaced by another and yet another until the whole shore became a grey swirling mass punctuated by orange points of explosions.

Then the assault began. The small landing-craft which had been huddling round the transport ships like chicks round a hen slowly drew away into formation heading for the shore. On the stroke of nine o'clock the barrage stopped and a few minutes later the first wave of soldiers was lost to sight in the smoke and debris of the plantations. The rattle of rifle and machine-gun fire echoed across the water of the bay as further waves of troops moved in, and soon the larger landing-ships nosed clumsily up the beach to disgorge tanks and lorries, guns and ammunition. I retired below for a drink of iced water.

In the middle of the afternoon we heard that our unit was to disembark at five o'clock. It was easy for us; we were able to walk down the ramp of our landing-ship straight on to the beach. The Air Force officers went off to find some of their lorries which were on another boat, and so Tony and I took charge of the forty-or-so airmen. Things soon started to go wrong. We were misdirected by a military policeman down a battered road and were met by a patrol coming back. 'Shouldn't go down there if I was you - the front line's down there.'

At six o'clock it grew dark (as everywhere on or near the Equator), and we turned into a palm-grove for the night. It was not a good choice because there was stagnant water nearby and the place was thick with mosquitoes despite having been sprayed from the air with D.D.T. Tony and I decided each to sleep for two hours

and watch for two hours while the other slept, with half a dozen sentries posted round the edge. Staring into the impenetrable mass of trees and undergrowth one was soon seeing all sorts of things which were not there, and life was made more uncomfortable by the sound of shots not far away. Dawn was the worst time because I was sure that we should be attacked then. Fortunately we were not, and was I glad to see mosquito nets again with men beneath them! Tony counted the number of mosquito bites on my back; there were over fifty, and that was through my shirt.

(We did not catch malaria because everyone had to take a yellow tablet of Atabrin three times a day, and these made your skin go yellow, so it was an easy job to see who was not taking them. We also had to take salt tablets regularly to replace the amount of salt we sweated out.)

Soon we found the others and eventually reached our permanent camp-site which was next door to the airfield. We had the whole camp to build in a day. I was responsible for the 'domestic arrangements', principally the latrines (loo) and the cook-house. The former consisted of a deep pit with a long raised wooden cover over it with large holes in it, and a canvas screen around. The latter was a place for the field-kitchen for cooking, and a sink made from half an oil-drum for washing up. All the water had to be brought by water-lorry because we could not trust the local stuff until it had been tested for purity. Six hours after construction began the cook had a hot meal prepared of bully-beef fritters, rehydrated potatoes, cabbage and carrots, followed by tinned stewed apple and custard, and, of course, tea, and he had had only four hours' sleep in the previous two nights. For the two days after landing we were each issued with a tin of emergency rations, enough for three days, nine meals in all; the contents were mainly dehydrated and compressed, like bully-beef, cereals, dates and raisins, with milk powder and, of course, tea. It was all right provided that there was plenty of water.

The ops tent was soon up and working, the messages started coming in, and we did our usual job of decoding and translating them and sending the results to Capt. Nave in Brisbane, though now by wireless. For the first week or two we were quite busy, but gradually activity tailed off. Few Japanese planes were flying in those parts because they were too busy north of the Philippines. Japan's main lifeline providing oil from Java, Sumatra and Borneo had now been decisively cut.

EXAMINING A CRASHED JAPANESE BOMBER ON LABUAN

The local battle went on for ten days, of which we were well aware because we had a battery of large guns, twenty-five pounders, firing shells over our heads against a cave where the surviving enemy were gathered. One night a hundred or so of them broke out and made their way to the beach by way of the airfield. Their officers used their swords and the men their bayonets because they had run out of ammunition, and several Australians and Americans were killed and wounded before the Japanese were finally overcome. They must have passed very near our tents.

We moved again, to our fourth site, and spent most of our energy making life more comfortable. We were next door to what had been the Governor's Residence where the flag-staff still stood in

63

the overgrown garden. The weather was stormy and one night Tony slept with three inches of water in his bed. We had a fine stream flowing through the tent, in at the front door and out at the back. So we planned to build up a wooden floor on posts and we cut down some young trees for the purpose. I realised then that they were rubber trees from what had been a plantation because when the bark was cut white latex oozed out. One night we went to the pictures in a clearing on the edge of the jungle, armed with revolvers, rifles and machine-guns just in case, and the film we saw was *The White Cliffs of Dover.*

On the third Sunday I went to a church service at a military hospital down the road, and as I came away a jeep passed carrying the chaplain and a medical colonel. Noticing my British cap they stopped to chat and asked if I would like to join them as they were going to a service for the locals who were mainly Chinese. I said, 'Yes, thanks', and we bumped along a primitive road to a large wooden house built, as usual, on stilts. Beneath was a table with a pure white cloth and two vases of beautiful orchids. There were fifty or sixty Christians there, from old men with wispy beards to young children running around as young children do. It was a most moving Communion service, straight from our English Prayer Book, with familiar English hymns, and only the sermon translated sentence by sentence into Chinese. I remember clearly that it was about the unchanging nature of the Gospel.

Afterwards we were invited to meet the head of the house. He gave us cups of tea and said that if we would like a banana to eat we were welcome to go outside and pick one. I was hesitant because they were green, but other people were eating them and so I followed suit and found they were delicious.

He told us of the terrible time they had had under the Japanese. All the clergy had been killed and church life had been kept going by the lay people. They met as and when they could, though it was dangerous, but they could not have Communion, and they had been looking forward to this for three years. Our host looked a rather austere man and the colonel asked him if he was married. He was. And did he have any children? 'Yes, eight.'

After another three weeks I received orders to join another Wireless Unit, No. 6, in the Philippines because there was not enough work to justify two of us in Labuan, and so bade farewell to my friends, and on 17th July took a plane by way of Morotai and Zamboanga to Manila, the capital city, where General MacArthur had his Headquarters.

CHAPTER 11

In the Philippines: San Miguel

Things may have been quiet in Borneo, but they certainly were not quiet north of the Philippines. Between April and June, 1945, the fight for the island of Okinawa, between Formosa (Taiwan) and Japan, was the largest and longest amphibious operation of the war. Four American divisions made the first landings and the Japanese garrison of over a hundred thousand men fought desperately. The remains of the Japanese navy, including the last surviving modern battleship, the *Yamato,* attempted to intervene, but were almost annihilated by American air power. The Americans landed an army of 450,000 men and 90,000 Japanese were reported killed. No fewer than 1,900 *kamikaze* attacks took place, sinking thirty-four destroyers and small craft and hitting about two hundred other ships. This was indeed a foretaste of what the final invasion of Japan would have been like. Mr Churchill himself foresaw the possible loss of a million American lives and half that number of British.

When I arrived in Manila on 17th July 1945 it was indeed a tragic sight. The city had been damaged when the Japanese captured it in early 1943, but it was devastated when the Americans recaptured it four months before my arrival. As I drove through it I felt very sorry for its people.

MANILA IN RUINS, JULY 1945

Our camp, a large American one, was about sixty miles north of Manila at a place called San Miguel (St Michael, pronounced San Migell), near Tarlac. We were on the edge of a large sugar plantation where they brewed alcohol from the sugar-cane. It was good to see ordinary people around the place again, and we were particularly glad because the Filipinos were willing to wash and iron our clothes for us at a small charge, and I felt very smart as a result.

I met up again with a number of friends, including one of the twelve, Peter Hall, who had been with No. 6 Wireless Unit since it arrived in the Philippines on the day after the first landings. The mainland of Japan was receiving a terrible pounding from American bombers based on the Marianas, a group of islands about 1500 miles south of Tokyo, and escorted by fighters from Iwo Jima, only half that distance away. I later learned that the great fire-bomb raids on Tokyo, a largely wooden city, killed more Japanese than did the atomic bomb on Hiroshima. General MacArthur was making his plans for the final invasion of Japan on the southern island of Kyushu (target date 1st November), and we were told that we were going to be the only non-American unit involved. I never did understand why his staff were so dissatisfied with the work of the equivalent American units. Fortunately for us, but not for the Japanese, the invasion never happened. On August 6th an American bomber dropped an atomic bomb on Hiroshima, wiping out the whole city-centre and killing some seventy thousand people, many of them women and children. We knew nothing about this weapon; the secret had been well kept.

Our wireless operators picked up the official war report from the Domei News Agency, and I had to translate it for General MacArthur. I still remember the words '*shingata bakudan*' which I took to mean 'new-type bomb', for the Japanese did not know what had hit them. The word 'shingata' was not in the dictionary, and my doubt was finally dispelled fifty years later in a television programme celebrating the anniversary of V-J Day. Taking part was a Japanese lady of about my age who was the daughter of a high government official at the time. She said she vividly remembered the announcement about the bomb, quoting it in Japanese, and then giving the translation.

One atomic bomb did not shake Japanese resolve and so, three days later, a second was dropped on Nagasaki, a great sea-port in the south of Japan. The day after that the Japanese government accepted an agreement to give up. I was in the Manila Hotel, having breakfast with an American officer-friend, when suddenly every ship in the harbour loosed off with its siren. We knew what that meant. The allied fleet sailed into Tokyo Bay and on 2nd September the formal surrender document was signed on the U.S. battleship *Missouri*. That night Manila went mad. We drove down to join in the fun. I can still see and hear the crowd and the shouting and the singing and the fireworks.

That was the end of the war. The one thought in everyone's head was 'How soon can I get home?', particularly for those who had served overseas for three or four years. We had only done a little over two and so we knew that we would not be among the first. (The armed services had to be demobilised slowly to allow people back into civilian life gradually.)

Having got so near to Japan some of us felt that we should go the whole way. One Australian army officer who shared my tent (there were six of us in one large tent) decided to hitch-hike there by air, and he caught a lift in a plane from the great American air-base at Clark Field. Unfortunately it crashed on landing at Tokyo and he was lucky to escape with his life, though he lost all his baggage. He also lost his cap, but enjoyed a few days in Tokyo, though he said it was largely in ruins and everyone was hungry and dirty. When he came back he had to go before the Colonel.

'I hear, Mr Price, that you have been hitch-hiking to Tokyo.'

'Yes, sir.'
'You know it's against orders, don't you?
'Yes, sir.'
'And you returned improperly dressed?'
'Yes, sir.'
'Well, Mr Price, just tell me how you did it. I want to go there myself next week.'

One of our British lads, Michael Webster, went one better and flew to China, to Chungking, though he was by no means certain about the return trip. When he was some days overdue we gave him up as lost, but he managed to re-appear ten days later.

I was more interested in learning how to drive a jeep, since all work had stopped. Our department had just been issued with six brand new ones (to the annoyance of the Americans) and we shared them out among the officers, one to a tent. We travelled for miles up and down the fine concrete roads which the Americans had built before the war, no doubt for strategic reasons. In due course I passed my army driving test, the only driving test I have ever passed, and an Australian one at that, and then I became an instructor. On one occasion we left the main road and got stuck in some mud in a kind of ford, but an obliging U.S. army lorry used its winch to pull us out. There was no trouble about petrol; one could pull up at any American unit by the road and they would fill you up with 'gas'.

We were able to pay a visit for a few days to an army rest-centre at Baguio, a summer resort five thousand feet up in the mountains, which made a pleasant change. It was cool and fresh, unlike San Miguel which was hot and steamy, and we had to light a fire in the evening and sleep with blankets. It must have been a beautiful town before the war, but now it was terribly battered. The weather was cloudy when we left, but on the way down it cleared and we had a wonderful view of the sea. The four of us were in good spirits and sang lustily until we came to a landslide. Fortunately the jeep is a handy vehicle (the name is reputed to come from 'G.P.' standing for 'General Purpose') and we got through where anything larger would have failed.

My other main recreation was with a delightful family who lived in a big house on the edge of the camp. Their name was Vidal (a common Spanish name) and papa was manager of the sugar-alcohol mill. The spirit which they offered us was real fire-water, about ninety-five per cent proof. They poured it into tiny glasses, and it had to be washed down with tumblers of water. They invited two of us to dinner and gave us roast chicken. It was small and not too tender, but it was fresh food, served on china plates on a clean white tablecloth, and it tasted wonderful. Señor Vidal had a wife, and her three younger sisters lived with them. The oldest was married, the youngest was a teenager, and the middle one, Estrella, was about my age. She was very attractive but very thin because she had had tuberculosis for most of the war and could get no medicine for it. She was a talented artist and gave me a picture she had painted for the cover of a magazine of a dark-skinned Filipino girl. She was not really allowed out but I did take her to the camp cinema one evening. It was lovely being among a family again.

The language there was Spanish because the Spaniards conquered the country after it had been discovered by Magellan in 1521. Many Spaniards settled there and married Filipinos so that

nearly everyone has a light brown complexion which is attractive. Estrella and her elder sister, I discovered, had been educated at a convent school in England and spoke remarkably good English. They told us of the grim time they had had under the Japanese. Estrella had been in hospital in Baguio recovering from pneumonia, and had to walk or be carried home down the mountains. Her elder sister in Manila had to walk through bombs and shells to get to a hospital to have her baby.

The camp had a fine chapel built by Filipino workmen using traditional materials, mainly bamboo, with a thatched roof, and I enjoyed singing in the choir which the Chaplain and his able lady assistant got together and trained. The Chaplain, who rejoiced in the name of Ira C. Hudgins, made quite an impression on me, and I can still remember long conversations with him about what I should study when I returned to Cambridge.

I even managed to get to a concert by the Manila Symphony Orchestra, which was a pretty good achievement on their part considering that a few months before most of the players had been guerrillas fighting the Japanese.

THE CAMP CINEMA

Many years after the end of the war I learned of one final comment about British translators. It came from Australia, firmly under MacArthur's direction, only a fortnight before Hiroshima. They asked for as many more Bedford students as possible: 'Could you indicate a possible figure and I shall initiate an official request. Your Bedford-trained translators most highly esteemed and would like as many as we may have: we can never have enough.'

THE CAMP CHAPEL, SAN MIGUEL

CHAPTER 12

Goodbye, Australia!

At the beginning of October a signal (wireless message) came through that we twelve were to leave the South-West Pacific Area for South-East Asia Command, though we could not imagine what they wanted us for; but we were not due to be released from the forces for at least another year. That meant going back to Australia to get dis-attached from the Australian Army (and Air Force).

In Manila harbour were two British aircraft-carriers and a Liberty cargo ship which between them were due to carry back to Brisbane not only all the Australian and British troops but also the Australians and British who had been prisoners-of-war of the Japanese for the last three years in that part of the world. In the event, the ex-prisoners went on the aircraft-carriers and on October 9th our party was put on board the Liberty ship, the S.S. *Francis N. Blanchet* of about 9,000 tons. She was lightly laden without much cargo, and tended to roll around when the weather was rough. When she dived down, the propeller used to come up out of the water and produce a mighty shuddering throughout the ship. The captain was a Norwegian who had learned his trade as a lad of fifteen 'before the mast' on a tall sailing-ship. The senior officers had the few cabins that there were, and the junior officers drew lots for what was left. I was lucky, getting the wheel-house which was light, airy and cool, and right away from the engines with their noise and smell.

FINSCHHAFEN, OCTOBER 1945

It was a pleasant cruise, lasting seventeen days. We had no work to do and the weather was mostly fine, hot sun by day, but always a cool breeze because of the ship's passage, with a bright tropical moon by night. We steamed south, then turned east, back past Morotai and Biak, and along the north coast of New Guinea, almost following the Equator. We had to call in at Finschhafen to put ashore a seaman who had appendicitis, but the place looked very quiet now, almost abandoned. We spent a lot of time sunbathing on deck wearing nothing but a handkerchief, and we got baked dark brown, though I did peel a little and ended up somewhat mottled. As far as I remember there was only one woman on board, but she seemed to cope.

My time was not entirely idled away. The Gunnery Officer, I discovered, had Gibbon's *Decline and Fall of the Roman Empire* in two large volumes, and I decided to read at least the first volume, which I did, and enjoyed it. Most evenings were spent playing bridge at which I became quite good.

The last part of the journey took us round the tail of New Guinea and through a heap of islands where, at one place, there was a channel only a mile and a half wide. Most of the islands are coral, with a great reef round each, sometimes many miles out, enclosing a lagoon of calm, emerald water lapping a brilliant yellow beach backed with palm trees. I thought about buying one such island and moving there.

Early in the morning of 27th October we steamed up the River to Brisbane to be greeted by a crisp, sunny spring day with a cool breeze blowing. The sprawling city made up for its wartime shabbiness by the blooming everywhere of the magnificent purple jacaranda trees which made a fine show on the hillsides. Most of the

No. 11 :

1 Tin Lard	16oz.
1 Tin Nestle's Malted Milk	16oz.
1 Tin Peanut Paste	16oz.
1 Pkt. Jelly	4oz.

Including Postage, 9/11

No. 12* :

1 Tin Cocoa Malt	4oz.
1 Bottle Ovaltine Tablets	3½oz.
1 Tin Globex Beef Extract	4oz.
1 Tin Libby's Lunch Beef	12oz.
3 Pkts. Jelly Crystals	4oz.
1 lb. Sugar	

Including Postage, 10/8

No. 13* :

1 Tin Horlick's Malted Milk	16oz.
½ lb. Tea	
1 lb. Sugar	
1 Tin Libby's Lunch Beef	12oz.
1 Pkt. Jelly Crystals	4oz.

Including Postage, 10/-

No. 14* :

1 Tin Honey	2lb.
1 Tin Lard	16oz.
½ lb. Tea	

Including Postage, 9/2

No. 15* :

1 Tin Honey	2lb.
½ lb. Tea	
1 lb. Sugar	
1 Bottle Bonox	2oz.

Including Postage, 9/9

* Require Coupons for Tea and Sugar.

No. 2 :

1 Ptk. Sultanas	16oz.
1 Pkt. Currants	16oz.
1 Pkt. Mixed Fruits	12oz.
1 Pkt. Custard Powder	16oz.
1 Pkt. Jelly Crystals	4oz.

Including Postage, 9/-

No. 3 :

1. Tin Nestle's Malted Milk	16oz.
1 Tin Peanut Paste	16oz.
1 Tin Marmalade	24oz.

Including Postage, 9/1

No. 4 :

1. Tin R.F. Camp Pie	16oz.
1 Tin Beef Sausages	16oz.
1 Tin Libby's Lunch Beef	12oz.
1 Tin Globex Beef Extract	8oz.

Including Postage, 10/4

No. 5 :

3 Jelly Crystals	4oz.
1 Mixed Fruit	12oz.
1 Libby's Lunch Beef	12oz.
1 Custard Powder	4oz.
1 Cocoa Malt	4oz.
1 Globex Beef Extract	4oz.
1 Ovaltine Tablets	3½oz.

Including Postage, 12/2

No. 7 :

1 Tin Lard	1lb.
1 Tin Peanut Paste	1lb.
1 Tin Milo	8oz.
1 Pkt. Custard Powder	4oz.
2 Pkts. Jelly Crystals	4oz.

Including Postage, 10/8

No. 8 :

1. Pkt. Sultanas	16oz.
1 Pkt. Currants	16oz.
1 Pkt. Mixed Fruits	12oz.
1 Pkt. Custard Powder	16oz.

Including Postage, 8/6

No. 9 :

1 Tin Sandwich Loaf (with Cereals)	12oz.
1 Tin Libby's Lunch Beef	12oz.
1 Pkt. Mixed Fruit	12oz.
1 Tin Cocoa Malt	4oz.
3 Pkts. Jelly Crystals	4oz.
1 Pkt. Custard Powder	4oz.

Including Postage, 10/3

No. 10 :

1 Tin Marmalade	24oz.
1 Pkt. Currants	16oz.
1 Tin Cocoa Malt	4oz.
1 Tin Libby's Lunch Beef	12oz.

Including Postage, 8/6

Americans had left, but there were quite a few British sailors and marines. I did not bump into anyone I knew.

I bought some new uniform (still tropical), sorted out and repacked a lot of possessions into a trunk which I bought, and went to the Food Department of Allan and Stark's, the big department store, where I saw my friend the manager and ordered a large food parcel to be sent home for Christmas.

The twelve of us now re-assembled for the first time since we arrived in Australia, and we all had become officers. One, Brian Warmington, had married an Australian wife. We lived from day to day until we received orders to proceed to India on 6th November by way of Sydney, Perth and Colombo. Barry Smallman managed to get sent back to Cambridge, and Brian Warmington, being unfit for tropical service, went home with his wife. Five flew on, but the rest of us had to wait. I did not mind at all but made straight for the Barkers who were pleased to put me up, though Mr Barker was away on business. He designed ships for the Australian Navy. I went to Tchaikovsky's opera *Eugene Onegin* at the Conservatorium (College of Music), and took Beatrice to a play *The Barretts of Wimpole Street*. She and her sister took me for a great trek through the bush ending up at a small backwater of the harbour with a dozen small boats. As the sun was setting, the clouds cleared and a brilliant light turned the water to a thick green, and the colour of the grass and the flowers was intense. I wrote to my parents suggesting that they should come out to Australia for a holiday, but they never did.

Owing to various delays with aeroplanes I managed to prolong my stay for a fortnight (which did not count as leave), and finally we left in a Liberator on 21st November, five officers with four warrant-officers who had come out later. We flew across the famous Nullarbor Plain where for a thousand miles there is just sandy desert with no sign of any green thing, only a railway line and an occasional house. I did not enjoy the flight because I became very air-sick, though I cannot imagine why because the flight was smooth and comfortable. Perhaps I had eaten too well in Sydney. I was extremely glad to land at Perth, and I soon recovered in the R.A.F. Officers' Mess. There was something wrong with our Liberator and so we had three days in Perth which enabled me to

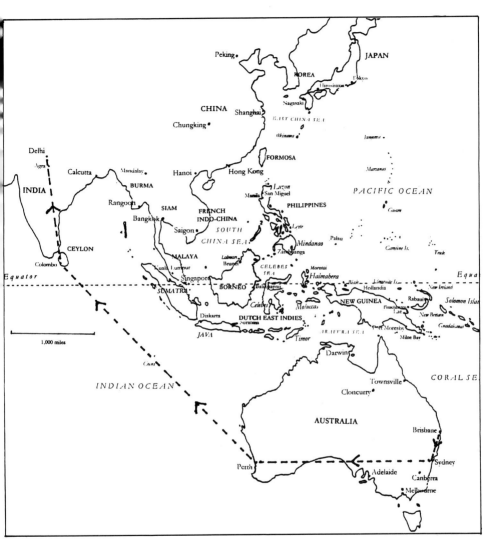

FROM BRISBANE TO DELHI

see a little of this beautiful city and its black swans. We finally set off, at the fourth attempt, at ten o'clock on the evening of 24th November and reached the Cocos Islands at 5.30 in the morning. This was a good time to be there because, after a wash and a shave, we sat along the beach and watched the rising sun tinge with pink the great surf breaking on the reef just off the shore. There was nothing else to see on that island apart from the airstrip, which had been built only a few months before, and, of course, coconut palms.

We left at half past eight in the morning and another nine hours' flying brought us to Colombo, Ceylon (now Sri Lanka) where we settled very comfortably in the Rifle Green Club. It was good to hear English being spoken again with all its many accents, and to see familiar regimental badges and flashes. For thirteen shillings a day, of which the Army paid ten, we had full board and lodging with a four-course dinner, shoes cleaned, clothes washed and starched, and one's every need attended to. I did a tour round the city in a rickshaw to check up on my financial position, and felt sorry for the poor Sinhalese man sweating as he pulled me.

I had the pleasure of meeting up again with an old Cambridge friend, a Sinhalese, Christie Eliezer, now holding a post in mathematics at Colombo University. He apologised for not inviting me to his home, but explained that his wife was expecting their first child at any moment, but we had a long conversation over numerous cups of tea about past times and times to come, including the possibility that he might return to Christ's as a Fellow. In the evening he took me to a concert at his University. On the Sunday I went to a service at Colombo Cathedral and heard a sermon which I can still remember clearly.

So off on the last leg to Delhi, to a new country, a new continent, and a new Command, South East Asia Command. My departmentt was the Intelligence Division of the Headquarters of the Supreme Allied Commander, Admiral Lord Louis Mountbatten, commonly known as SACSEA.

CHAPTER 13

Delhi, India

My unit was now SEATIC, the South-East Asia Translator and Interpreter Corps, and we lived and worked in New Delhi, seven miles from the old city. It was a striking monument to British rule in India, designed by Sir Edwyn Lutyens. A fine road, two miles long, rose up a gradual slope to the splendid Viceroy's House at the

top. This was flanked on either side by government offices in which we worked. At the bottom end of the road were some modern barracks where we lived in rather grand style. We had comfortable bedrooms, with Indian servants ('bearers') to look after us, make our beds and clean our shoes, and a pleasant mess with Indian waiters. Unfortunately all this luxury resulted in large mess bills which

meant that I could not save much money. Up till then I had saved nearly all my pay because in the bush there was nothing to spend it on except soap, toothpaste a n d talcum powder. Never mind, it was worth it for a change.

The weather was sunny but cold enough (it was December and we had now returned to the northern hemisphere) to warrant wearing battle-dress for the first time in eighteen months, and we enjoyed a fire in the evening. We also enjoyed being able to send and receive full air letters by air mail instead of the weekly one-sheet airgraphs or air-letter forms, and these took six or seven days. I was also delighted to receive a weekly newspaper printed on very thin paper, also by air mail, and so I was able to pick up again the strings of what was going on in the wide world. England was trying to get used to a Labour government under Mr Attlee and was facing enormous economic difficulties because much of its wealth had gone into fighting the war, and America had stopped most of its wartime aid. It was only now that I learned that I had not been selected for the Australian Diplomatic Service. I was not surprised and not really sorry because I was looking forward to going back to Cambridge, and had nearly decided to read medicine, but regretted my total lack of science.

NINE OF THE TWELVE, NEW DELHI, DECEMBER 1945
Left to right: Peter Hall, John Smart, Bernard Bellingham, Ray Eddolls, Rupert Fenn (behind), Michael Webster, Bennie Polack, Donald Fletcher, Cyril James

Work was not a serious problem. The badge of our Headquarters, which we wore on our shoulders, was a rectangle, blue at the bottom and red at the top with a gold star in the middle, interpreted as 'the star of India rising out of a sea of ink into a sky

80

of red tape' (the latter being used to tie up bundles of official documents). I heard that there were some Japanese prisoners-of-war in Delhi and I thought it would be a good idea to learn to speak the language as well as write it. I was given permission to go to the prison in the Red Fort in Old Delhi twice a week, and was introduced to one Captain Agano who told me that he had been a solicitor in Tokyo before the war. He was very polite, and kept bowing and hissing at me which in Japan is a great courtesy. It did not, however, make for good teaching because he was terrified of correcting me for fear of having his head cut off for insubordination. He knew some English but we did not have any text books and so we had to make everything up as we went along. I did discover that his spoken Japanese was pretty different from the written language that we had been working with. He gave me the impression of being a charming and cultivated man who could hold his own in any educated society. I think he learned more English than I did Japanese.

We celebrated Christmas 1945 in traditional style with a cocktail party in the mess on Christmas Eve and two enormous dinners the next day when we waited on the men at the first, and they waited on us at the second. A couple of the men dressed up as the Brigadier and his Aide-de-camp doing a ceremonial inspection of the meal. When the real Colonel came along there were some amusing fireworks.

Talking of colonels, the Supremo himself, Lord Louis in person, paid us a visit, presented His Excellency the Viceroy with a captured 150mm. gun, and dined in our mess. I also had the peculiar experience of attending a conference of staff officers (of which I was not one) addressed by the Adjutant General, General Sir Robert Adam, on the 'Administration of the British Army as Seen from the Top'. Amid the welter of top brass and red tabs I was the only subaltern there. I felt very, very small. My view of the army's organisation as seen from the bottom was that my pay arrangements had broken down so that I could not pay my bearer or my mess bills which was rather embarrassing.

A fortnight after Christmas I was sitting on the grass outside my room with a cup of afternoon tea and some sandwiches when a great vulture dive-bombed me from the rear and, neatly

81

manoeuvring between my left ear and the teapot, removed a half-eaten sandwich from the plate. Peter Hall's bearer who was sitting on the verandah-step opposite, polishing Peter's shoes (his main occupation) was not a little shaken by the sight of this great bird climbing sharply a foot or two in front of his nose.

A few days later, the pianist Solomon gave a recital in the Viceroy's House (which in any other country would have been a Palace). We swept up the long drive, climbed an imposing flight of steps, passed into the throne-room whose floor was solid marble, and thence into the ballroom whose walls and ceiling were richly decorated with imperial paintings. After the concert, while eating a vice-regal sandwich or two, I met a corporal in the A.T.S. (Auxiliary Territorial Service) who had been reading Classics at Newnham College during my year. I invited her to dinner the next evening and we had a long and pleasant chat about old times.

SEATIC was clearly running down and they had a job to find enough translating for us to do, when the Colonel proposed a new post for me. A plan was afoot to re-educate the large number of Japanese in Singapore who had surrendered at the end of the war. This sounded interesting as it would have meant promotion, with some interesting possibilities for the future. Sadly it came to nothing, and I heard nothing more about it even when I finally moved to Singapore.

There was one treat I was determined to have, and that was to visit the Taj Mahal at Agra, a town about 110 miles south of Delhi. This building was ordered in 1630 by the Mogul Emperor

Shah Jehan as a magnificent burial place for his favourite wife
Mumtaz-i-Mahal. Michael Webster and I managed to secure a long
week-end off duty, took a train to Agra, and with some difficulty
found accommodation in a comfortable hotel. I had been told that
you *must* see the Taj Mahal for the first time by moonlight because
it is made of white marble, and in moonlight it glistens like magic.
So we had dinner and then walked to it. There was a bright moon
and the sight was breath-taking. The night was warm and still, and
there was this lovely building with its graceful dome and four
minarets shimmering silver-white against a velvety black sky. I gazed
at it for an hour or more. It was hard to tear oneself away and go
back to the hotel and bed.

The next morning I went again and enjoyed more fully the
distant view of it from the far end of a long pool of water which
provided beautiful reflections. The inside of the building was a riot
of colour with all sorts of precious stones inlaid in the surface of the
marble.

We were not encouraged to go into Old Delhi because the
British Army was not too popular with the Indians. Although we
had prevented the Japanese from invading India by the long, grim
war in Burma, the Indians were thirsting after independence, and
British soldiers meant for them the British Empire which they
wanted to be rid of. However, I did pay one visit to Old Delhi with
a friend, saw the famous Red Fort, and visited some shops, but did
not find much to buy.

There was so little work to do that they decided to send me to Singapore. So I packed my bags again and on 23rd January 1946, having stayed just long enough to see John Gielgud play *Hamlet*, took off about midday in a Dakota. The journey should have lasted

about 36 hours, but we could not land at Calcutta because of riots in the city, and were diverted to an aerodrome nearly a hundred miles away where we had to spend the night. We did not leave till 2.30 p.m. the next day and so we arrived at Pegu (outside Rangoon, Burma) that evening after dark. There were about six of us, in addition to a lot of freight, and our number included a classic B.B.C. type with long hair, suede shoes, a superb Roman nose and a generally blasé manner. There was also one woman, and at Pegu, in the rough mess there with jungle twenty or thirty feet away, a lady in a smart costume with silk (or rayon) stockings and all her bags and chattels including a tennis racquet, appeared slightly incongruous. I had clearly not yet adjusted myself to peacetime living.

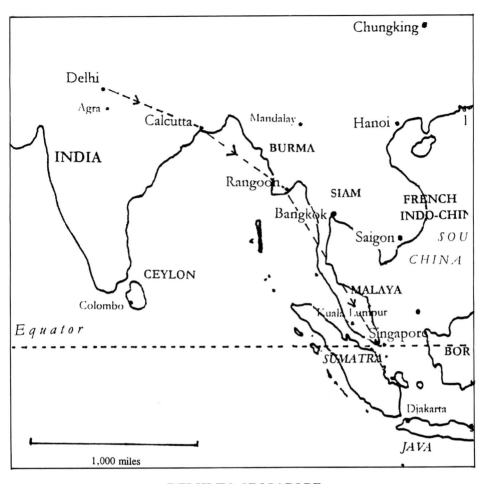

DELHI TO SINGAPORE

We had to get up at half-past five the next morning, but take-off was delayed because of a heavy mist, and so I took a constitutional several times up and down the airstrip. We got off at ten and descended for lunch at Butterworth (Penang). Then it suddenly dawned on me that it was January 25th: so passed my twenty-second birthday. The journey was not made more comfortable by the fact that I was carrying some thirty thousand rupees worth of bullion (presumably gold) for which I had signed. I was glad to hand it over to the proper authorities at the end of the journey.

CHAPTER 14

Singapore

Singapore had not been badly damaged because we had recaptured it without a fight. The Japanese had occupied it for nearly three years, using it as an important naval and air base (it had three airfields, and there were still many (I was told 40,000) prisoners-of-war working there on roads, buildings and in the fields. Conditions were so bad in Japan, with little food, clothing or power, that they were only allowed home gradually. They looked very sorry for themselves but they worked hard. There was not much in the shops as the Japanese had taken everything worth while, but I managed to buy some Thai silk as a late wedding present for my sister Joan.

I lived with three other army officers in a rather grand house in Bukit Tima Road with a large garden including a very English sundial on a stone pedestal. The Chinese gardener was beginning to get it back into order. One of my companions was a Captain Brain who later became a Member of Parliament, but I do not think he ever quite lived up to his name.

There did not seem much chance of my returning to Cambridge in 1946. In February I received a letter from my Senior Tutor stating that I was Number 133 on the College's priority list, whereas so far only the first twenty-five had returned. There was talk of part of our section going to Australia, and I would have been happy to spend another year there. I also applied for a posting to Japan for intelligence duties with the British occupation forces, but that came to nothing. In the event things worked out differently.

Singapore was hot, which was not surprising since it was almost on the Equator. There was no summer or winter; it was hot and wet all the year round. Every day the sun rose at six in the morning and set at six in the evening. Every afternoon it rained, but the evenings were beautiful. We used to sit out on the patio in the moonlight listening to the bull-frogs croaking loudly at the bottom of the garden. I became very fond of drinking iced gin-and-lime (the gin being cheaper than the lime-juice) accompanied by Beethoven's Violin Concerto, because Major Money upstairs used to play it on

an old gramophone he had acquired, and left the window open. Whenever I hear it now, I am carried back to those tropical nights. Every evening I read Tolstoy's novel *War and Peace* and finished it in six weeks - it is a long book.

Life was comfortable. We had Chinese 'boys' (young men) to cook and clean for us and wait at table. One of them caught me consulting a Japanese dictionary and offered to teach me Chinese (many of the characters being the same) but the prospect of having to learn the different tones which went with each character put me off. I wore shirt and shorts and shoes with long woollen socks. We normally had to change our shirts at midday because they would be drenched with perspiration. My feet did not like wool because it was too hot, and I developed 'athlete's foot', sores between the toes. I went to the army doctor who tried painting them with all sorts of brightly-coloured liquids, including gentian violet, which did no good. Eventually I went to a naval doctor who said 'The cure is simple. Bathe them in salt water as often as you can, in the sea if you like.' I did, and in a few days they were mended.

We had our diversions, one of which arose from a swarm of bees which formed on the side of the house under a gutter. They started going into the upstairs room of a colonel, and so the 'boys' decided to burn them out with a long pole surmounted by some inflammable matter. This they did, and the infuriated bees went into another colonel's room downstairs, next to mine, and he got out from beneath his mosquito net with next to nothing on to see what all the commotion was about. Unfortunately he stepped out with his bare feet on to a mass of flaming bees, and emerged from his room in a towel and the wildest temper I have ever seen. We all

sought protection in the weirdest dress, and a naval sub-lieutenant, about six feet five in height and fifteen stone in weight, tried to hide in my wardrobe. Almost speechless with rage, the colonel said to the other colonel: 'Go to bed: that's an order!' and received the reply, 'Don't be so silly'. We were exploding with laughter.

Our office was a pleasant place, on the third floor of the Cathay Building, the tallest building in the city, sited on a hill in the centre and only completed in 1939, with a striking outlook over the harbour. I had very agreeable colleagues; our senior officer was one Major Phillips, by origin a Polish Jew, born in Glasgow, married to an Indian wife, fluent in half a dozen languages, and possessed of a schoolboyish humour. Then there was Captain Padfield who had degrees in Hebrew, Aramaic, and Theology, had done twelve months as a motor-cycle dispatch-rider, had a great fund of good stories, and was one of the most unaffected men I have ever met. There was also a naval Sub-lieutenant and a Flight Officer in the W.A.A.F. for good measure.

Work? They found enough to keep us moderately busy. My job was to help compile a Japanese 'Order of Battle' from captured documents: that is to find out where every unit of their army was at the time of surrender. Quite often the Japanese did not know themselves because their communications had largely broken down. This was in preparation for the writing of a history of the war in the Far East on which Major Money was starting. He expected to go on with this in England and he asked me if I would like to join him. 'Sorry, chum,' I replied, 'I want to go back to Cambridge and finish my degree.' He was disappointed.

The communists were active and noisy. Pandit Nehru came from India to pay a visit to Lord Mountbatten, and many demonstrations were held in his honour. We saw the Chinese flag, the Indian Congress one, the Indonesian, and the Red Banner, but not a single Union Jack. This was an omen of trouble to come.

In April 1946 we heard the first news of LIAP (leave in advance of Python where Python stood for repatriation). This meant twenty-eight days' home leave for those who had served abroad for two years or more, in order of priority for length of service. I put in my application.

On Sundays I went to the service in Singapore Cathedral which looked much like an English one apart from the rotating fans to provide some cooling. We used the English Prayer Book, and I soon discovered that the Japanese had cut out every page which contained prayers for the King. I think that for a time they closed the place for worship and used it for some other purpose. The Bishop of Singapore and other clergy spent the war in the notorious Changi Gaol where they were very badly treated. Towards the end, their total food ration was six ounces of rice a day and water, and if their captivity had not ended when it did they would have died of starvation. One of the clergy held there was Eric Cordingly who had

89

been a Senior Chaplain among the English and Australian prisoners-of-war whom the Japanese compelled to build the Burma-Siam railway. He later became the Bishop of Thetford and I got to know him well. He said that he could never eat a large meal again because his stomach had shrunk permanently.

A typical sung Eucharist took place at seven o'clock on Sunday morning with something like a hundred and fifty communicants, less than half of whom, including service people, were European. The Dean usually presided, assisted by two curates, who I think were Malayan but may have been Chinese, and a young woman at the organ. The choir embraced Chinese boys and girls, Malays and Europeans with some servicemen. The congregation was colourful, from the white of the navy to the khaki of the army with civilian men mainly in white and their ladies in bright dresses; the Chinese ladies wore their brilliantly-coloured silk pyjama-style suits, while the Indian women sported their best silk saris in purple or green or blue or yellow. On one occasion the service ended with a monumental storm; the thunder roared, the lightning cracked, and the rain came down in sheets so that the cathedral was darkened; it felt quite English.

A few days earlier I had remarked to a friend that since I had been abroad I had only met one person I knew. Ten minutes later, a naval lieutenant walked across and said he remembered me from Christ's where we had argued fiercely in the debates of the Milton Society, and I remembered his name, Crellin. He invited me to a meal at the Naval Base at Johore Bahru and later took me on a tour of the docks including the dry dock which I was told was the second biggest in the world, next only to Sydney. Then we went to a performance of *Messiah,* superbly sung by an expanded Welsh choir. He was engaged in a voluntary education scheme, learning Malay and German (he found some German prisoners from the U-boats which had been based in Singapore) and instructing in Higher Maths and Physics.

On May 3rd I wrote home to say that my LIAP leave had been granted and, after various false alarms, I sent a telegram home on May 24th saying that I should arrive about 17th June, and embarked on His Majesty's Troopship *Corfu.* I expected to come back to Singapore and left a trunk of my belongings behind. The

90

journey was a leisurely one of twenty-five days, across the Indian Ocean, up the Red Sea, through the Mediterranean, round Spain and into Tilbury Docks, London. So I was to complete the round trip.

On the ship a British officer, Captain Don Laidlaw, organised a bridge four, and we played bridge morning, noon, and night until I was really rather good at the game. Life in the Red Sea was very hot, too hot even for bridge - we just had to sweat it out. We called in at Alexandria to renew supplies, but we were not allowed off the ship. That was our only stop.

So finally we caught sight of England as we entered the Channel, and at last sailed up the Thames to dock at Tilbury. Soon we were off the ship and on to the train. I phoned home to say when I was arriving and my father came to meet me on the platform of East Croydon station. We embraced warmly and soon I was home. After an hour or two the whole adventure seemed quite unreal. How could I have been right round the world when there I was eating my mother's familiar cakes at tea?

To celebrate my home-coming my parents had arranged a car tour of several days to the west country, for which my father had carefully saved up his petrol coupons. A school-friend of his had just become Bishop of Bath and Wells, and the end-point of our journey was a visit to him in his moat-girt palace (with swans) where he laid on a magnificent strawberry and cream tea. That seemed totally unreal! How could it be in the same world as Darwin or Labuan or the Philippines?

The leave was two weeks in June and two in July, and there were many parties and much meeting up with friends and relations and hearing how they had all fared over the previous two years. Some, like Nobby Clark, had not come back. His ship had been torpedoed in the Atlantic and all the officers were killed in the explosion. I went to see his parents in Croydon. He was their only child upon whom they had built all their hopes and with his death the bottom had dropped out of their world. Another member of my sixth-form, Gus Roberts, had been killed in the R.A.F. I was fortunate.

To hasten my special release to the University I went to the War Office and in a dusty room found a dusty Major who dug out a dusty file with some papers about me. He blew the dust off to look through them and found a form headed 'Record of Service'. It was blank. 'Where have you been for the last couple of years?', he enquired. I told him. 'Be a good chap, take this home, fill it up and let me have it back.' That was all they knew about my wanderings.

CHAPTER 15

Kensington Palace Gardens

The Major could not have been all that dusty because half way through my leave a letter arrived from the War Office with the good news that my special Class B Release would come through in time for me to return to Christ's College in October. In the meantime I would not go back to Singapore but was to report to No. 6 Kensington Palace Gardens in the heart of London.

'What's all this about?', I wondered. To make me feel more the part I bought myself an officer's service dress, put on my Sam Browne belt and my old peaked cap which had accompanied me faithfully round the world, and went into battle on a train from East Croydon station, for I continued to live at home.

The unit was War Crimes Interrogation Unit and its Commanding Officer was Lieutenant-Colonel Scotland, a mild-looking elderly gentleman with white hair and a slightly untidy appearance, looking like a retired country solicitor. His task was to obtain information about crimes committed by senior German commanders, mainly against civilians or prisoners-of-war, and I soon learned that he was the terror of their armed forces. His staff of Intelligence Corps officers and sergeants were all fluent speakers of German and several other European languages, and they scoured the corners of Europe, even the sewers of Vienna, for criminals who might be hiding there or for evidence which could lead to their arrest or be used at their trial. Only later did I learn that Colonel Scotland had served in the First World War posing as a German officer on the German General Staff and passing valuable information to England.

In the grounds of this large house in Kensington Palace Gardens was a cage of barbed wire inside which were huts forming a prison where senior German officers were watched over by a company of Coldstream Guards. I was once talking with Colonel Scotland in his office when I heard someone come in, stop and click his heels. I turned round and found myself facing Field Marshal von Runstedt, who had commanded the German Army in France in

1944; another time I saw Field Marshal Keitel who had signed the surrender document in Berlin and Grand-Admiral Doenitz who had master-minded the U-boat war and had been appointed to succeed Hitler after his death. All of them appeared in the dock at the Nuremberg War Crimes Trial.

Early in the war, in 1940, a company of the Royal Norfolk Regiment was captured in France. The German commander marched them into a cornfield and gave orders to machine-gun the lot. Nearly all were killed, but two, though wounded, pretended to be dead and later managed to crawl away. They were, however, captured again and spent the rest of the war in a prison camp. Colonel Scotland vowed that he would find the German officer who had committed this crime, and managed to trace one of the survivors. From his story the Colonel succeeded in tracking down the officer who duly received his sentence at Nuremberg.

As I could not speak German I was no use to their intelligence gathering. My job was Administrative Officer and I spent my time filling in forms and making sure that everyone received his pay and allowances. I was told that Colonel Scotland was so highly valued by the government that he was allowed to draw money directly from the Treasury without having to render accounts.

A major task of mine was making peace with the Guards sergeant-major in charge of the building because the Intelligence Corps staff were a pretty casual lot of soldiers who could not be bothered to keep the place tidy. For the Guards everything had to be in place, squared up, and if possible polished. That did not go down at all well with the I. Corps. But we managed to live together.

I joined that unit in July 1946 when I also bought a season ticket for the Promenade Concerts at the Albert Hall, price one guinea, which gave me a seat for every concert for eight weeks in the 'gods', the top balcony which had rather hard wooden chairs. I only had to walk across Kensington Gardens, past the statue of Peter Pan, and I was there. So I feasted myself on real music, having heard very little for three years.

The Proms finished in early September, and so does this story. I wrote my own discharge on 11th September, but had paid leave until 2nd October when it was time to go back to Cambridge. Which is where this tale began, three years and forty-six thousand miles ago.

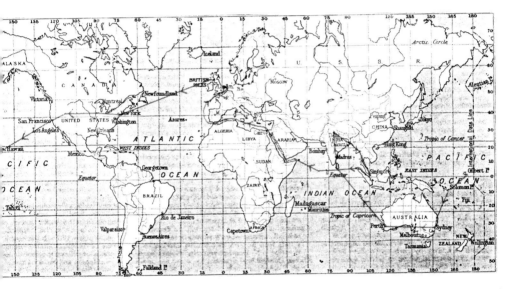

THE ROUND TRIP

FOR FURTHER READING

Bleakley J., *The Eavesdroppers*, Canberra, Australian Government Publishing Service, 1991.

Calvocoressi P., *Top Secret Ultra,* Cassell, 1980.

Costello J., *The Pacific War,* Collins. 1981.

Hinsley F.H. et al., *British Intelligence in the Second World War* (4 vols.) H.M.Stationery Office, 1979-88.

Hinsley F.H. and Stripp A., *Codebreakers,* Oxford University Press, 1993.

Jones R.V., *Most Secret War: British Intelligence 1939-45,* Hamish Hamilton, 1978.

Kahn D., *The Codebreakers,* Weidenfeld and Nicholson, 1966.

Kirby S.W. et al., *The War Against Japan* (5 vols.), H.M. Stationery Office, 1959-69.

Lewin R., *The Other Ultra,* Hutchinson, 1982; also known as *The American Magic,* Penguin, 1983.

Ocean Front: The Story of the War in the Pacific 1941-1944, H.M.Stationery Office, 1945

Rusbridger J. and Nave E., *Betrayal at Pearl Harbour,* O'Mara, 1991.

Stripp A., *Codebreaker in the Far East,* Cass, 1989.